EVANGELICALS in the WHITE HOUSE: The CULTURAL MATURATION of BORN AGAIN CHRISTIANITY 1960-1981

Evangelicals in the
White House:
The Cultural Maturation
of Born Again Christianity
1960-1981

BY

ERLING JORSTAD

STUDIES IN AMERICAN RELIGION
VOLUME FOUR

THE EDWIN MELLEN PRESS
NEW YORK AND TORONTO

Library of Congress Cataloging in Publication Data

Jorstad, Erling, 1930–
    Evangelicals in the White House.

    (Studies in American religion; v. 4)
    Includes bibliographical references.
    1. Evangelicalism--United States--History--
20th century. 2. Presidents--United States--
Religion. I. Title. II. Series.
BR1642.U5J67   280'.4   81-9674
ISBN 0-88946-881-8 (soft)   AACR2
ISBN 0-88946-982-2 (hard)

Studies in American Religion   ISBN 0-88946-992-X

            The Edwin Mellen Press
            P.O. Box 450
            Lewiston, New York 14092

"The Chicago Declaration, November 1973" has been reprinted from
The Chicago Declaration, edited by Ronald J. Sider, copyright
1974, by permission of Creation House.

Printed in the United States of America

Other books by the author:

The Politics of Doomsday:
Fundamentalists of the Far Right

Love it or Leave It?
A Dialog on Loyalty

That New-Time Religion:
The Jesus Revival in America

The Holy Spirit in Today's Church

Bold in the Spirit:
Lutheran Charismatic Renewal in America

The New Politics of Moralism:
The New Christian Renewal in America

ACKNOWLEDGMENTS

My thanks go to the American Lutheran Church and the Faculty Development Award Program at the place of my employment, St. Olaf College, for financial support. Just as important, thanks beyond words go to those persons at Holden Village, a lay renewal center near Chelan, Washington, for their support. Most of this book was written there where I experienced in the idyllic setting of the North Cascades what life in community means. Some day I will return there to do double duty to atone for the number of times I missed "dishteam" duties so I could work on this manuscript. The Villagers were a loving support system unique to my experience, and in gratitude I dedicate this work to them. When in doubt or apathy over seeing it to completion, the Village slogan for the year led me to complete it; that slogan was "go for it." I cannot resist suggesting to the reader that they go for it by spending some time there: Holden Village, Chelan, Washington 98816.

CONTENTS

PART ONE

THE EVANGELICAL TRADITION REFORMED, 1945-1975

PART TWO

HARVEST OF STALEMATE: EVANGELICALS DIVIDED, 1976-1980

PART THREE

THE YEARS OF THE EVANGELICALS: AMERICAN REVIVALISM, 1976-1980

PART FOUR

EVANGELICALS IN THE WHITE HOUSE

APPENDIX I

PART ONE

THE EVANGELICAL TRADITION REFORMED

1945-1975

.

CHAPTER I

THE CULTURAL MATURATION OF
BORN AGAIN CHRISTIANITY

The religious revival is one of the most original contributions to Christianity made by the American people. Nowhere else in Protestant Christendom have revivals been so widespread and accepted by so many believers as normal religious expression. Throughout their history in this country, revivals have taken on a set of expectations and characteristics by both participants and observers; everyone, to their own satisfaction, knows what a revival is.

In the late 1970s, America underwent yet one more religious revival. Its form and substance reflected its debt to earlier movements, yet it had, as all revivals do, its own distinctive personality. It was a revival in that, as defined by Prof. William G. McLoughlin, Jr., "charismatic evangelists convey 'the Word of God' to large masses of people who, under this influence, experience what Protestants call conversion, salvation, regeneration, or spiritual rebirth."[1] Its distinctive characteristics emerged out of the useful differentiation made by McLoughlin between revivals and "awakenings". "The latter are periods of cultural revitalization that begin in a general crisis of beliefs and values and extend over a period of a generation or so, during which time a profound reorientation in beliefs and values take place. Revivals alter the lives of individuals; awakenings alter the world view of a whole people or culture."[2]

The revival of 1976 to 1981 can best be understood by keeping the distinctions between these two movements in mind. Revival there was, in abundance, but it appeared as one expression of the larger awakening across the nation starting somewhere in the early 1960s. The awakening in its fullest expression assumed a life quite unexpected and certainly unprecedented in American history. As will be discussed in Part Four, the born again Christians broke out of their traditional role of indifference to or hostility to organized politics. They participated fully in the several revival-type activities (described in Parts Two and Three), but as both a culmination of past movements and as a harbinger of things to come, the evangelicals reached a level of cultural maturation through their involvement in national elective politics that gave the entire movement, from 1960 to 1981, the characteristics of both an awakening and a revival.

The awakening and the backlash against it focused on themes such as liberation (black, women's, ethnic), disenchantment with existing governing institutions (government, schools, churches, business world), and renewal of the primacy of individual autonomy and concerns (spirituality, the charismatic renewal, cults, the human potential movement).

The revival of the late 70s stood as one phase of the larger awakening. As I will argue, it attempted to hold fast to the traditional expectations of earlier revivals, yet it turned out to be so strongly shaped by the larger awakening that it took on a personality all its own. To date, no student of this movement has probed in depth the historical roots, the inner tensions, and the extent of popular participation in this revival. This book seeks to fill that need. [3]

Our attention in this work centers almost exclusively on the revival; for the larger setting of the awakening the readers are invited to pursue those works which embrace a larger perspective. [4] What stands out so vividly today about the most recent revival is that it did not (and I will argue, cannot) escape the many controversies ensnarling everyone caught up in revival over the centuries of American history. Among these, the most crucial for revivalists has centered around the question of whether Christianity was in essence either (1) a set of transcendent, redeeming doctrines based on the life and accounts of its founders which speak by themselves sufficiently to the spiritual life of each new generation; or (2) whether those Christian truth claims need to be brought up to date by each generation in light of new biblical and scientific research, by changing societal problems, or by shifting norms of morality. Over the decades, most revivalists have lived somewhere between these two poles. Yet the basic tension between them has not been resolved, and indeed continues down to our day.

This tension can be rephrased in biblical terminology. Seekers are exhorted both to "hold fast what is good" (I Thess. 5:21) and to "press on towards the goal for the prize" (Phil. 3:14). Most revivalists uphold the first position--the more "conservative" one. Yet the second position--the more "radical"--calls for pressing on, for seekers to find new ways to understand and apply God's commands for one's newborn life lived out in a constantly changing world.

What is remarkable about the revival of the 1970s is that, by contrast to earlier ones in which the holders fast prevailed, now the pressers on have achieved prominence enough to transform revivalism itself. So deep and pervasive has the division between the two camps become that we can conclude that the revivalists tradition in America has reached a stalemate with no apparent resolution in sight.

This impasse is more than a little ironic. Evangelicals (as defined below) have enjoyed a certain strength and influence within American Christendom because of their internal agreement on the essentials of their faith. By contrast to those outside their camp, they preserved their own identity with remarkable unity. Equally ironic is the fact that just as it seemed in the late 1970s that their numbers and influence would propel them into the mainstream of American religious life,[5] enjoying an influence never known before, they broke into often acrimonious division over the specific issues stemming from the holding-pressing impasse.

Hence, the present day can be seen as a fruitful time to look in some detail, at this, the most recent revival. By a careful examination of its major contours, we may gain a better map of where this way of life may be headed. In other words, we will be looking at both its past (which as an historian I am trained to do) and at its future (which as a student of religious life I find necessary). Critics may justly argue the historian should be concerned only with the past; my response would be that unless the past suggests the road ahead in a movement which may, in the judgment of at least two careful observers, rescue America from its current malaise, an account of its past would be of antiquarian interest only.[6]

To convince the reader that the revivalist-evangelical tradition has reached its impasse and at the same time a new cultural maturation, I offer four interpretive theses as organizing threads for holding together the many strands of the story. First: a revival, documentable and influential in American life, did occur in these years. Contrary to what its critics stated, this was more than a media event. Second: by contrast to earlier revivals, in this one the pressers on captured the initiative. Their break with the holders fast, especially over the questions of Biblical inerrancy and specific social questions, virtually destroyed any foreseeable prospect for evangelicals being able to speak, as they had in the past, as one voice in American religious life. Three: the true center of this revival is better understood to have taken hold the most vigorously on the local and popular level of understanding. This last achievement has been overlooked largely by earlier students of this revival; they have kept the spotlight on the debates between holders and pressers in the seminaries, colleges, and church think tanks. While major transformations within the tradition may well result from these controversies, the immediate impact of the revival was most clearly found not in academia but in the everyday lives of the reborn. Fourth: as if the scholarly impasse and the popular revival were not enough to break evangelicals out of their traditional role in American Protestantism, they extended the revival into an awakening by unprecedented, spirited participation in the national political campaign of 1980. For decades, even centuries, evangelicals had refrained from such involvement, preferring one to one evangelism. Now, at decade's end, they showed to the surprise of everyone except themselves how sophisticated, organized and pragmatic they could be in using the election of specific candidates to further their specific tenets of morality. When these four theses are placed alongside one another, they add up to the conclusion that American evangelicalism is a new creature.

To convince the reader that these theses are useful ways of understanding this revival, we need at the outset to define terms. Otherwise, we could all well be lost in a sematic thicket, each trying to bushwack one's way out by his own efforts. "Revival" and "awakening" have already been defined clearly by McLoughlin. But the term "evangelical" has already crept into this text without definition. Few terms in religious vocabulary are more elusive, yet necessary to define carefully. Before 1976 we could say with confidence that evangelicals constituted a definable, articulate movement within American Protestantism. That was possible because evangelicals were set apart by (1) there trust in the efficacy of an instant, historically identifiable moment of conversion, occurring as often as not during a planned revival; (2) their insistence on the absolute authority of the Bible. By that they meant that the Bible alone (and hence not personal experience, church councils or manmade theology) defines the character of the Christian faith; and (3) their trust in the efficacy of propositional doctrine. The Bible taught clear, logical, defensible doctrines which when properly organized constituted the essence of the Christian faith. In the words of two historians: "Instead of statements reflecting an experience of encounter with truth, truth now was tantamount to the statement itself. Hence, theological formulations became the norm of Christian truth, including that of the experience of God through the Bible."[7]

Many Protestants standing outside this definition have insisted that their particular loyalties and commitments qualify them for the title of "evangelical". This has been especially true for many churches of the early Reformation (Lutheran, Presbyterian, Anglican) because of their higher priority than today's evangelicals to the liturgy, formal worship and precisely defined structures of church government. And, when historical precedence is claimed by these groups for the title of evangelical, the case is well taken. However, following Martin E. Marty, I submit that we have to let people call themselves what they want to be called. Those who are the subjects of this book want to be called "evangelicals" and so it is used for them as a working label.[8]

Today's evangelicals, divided as they are, stand apart from the early Reformation definition because of their insistence that the Bible is the absolute, sole authority in every question, dispute, or other area of uncertainty in religious faith. That conviction results from their commitment (far more pronounced than in other Protestant bodies) to the doctrines of verbal inspiration and the infallibility and inerrancy of Scriptures.[9]

So, as this book will argue, the term "evangelical" in its popular sense holds to the pre-1970s definition, but one major addition has been contributed by the pressers on. That is the conviction that in examining questions of Biblical interpretation and major social issues, believers can and should add to the Biblical authority the appropriate findings of scholarship in such fields as anthropology, linguistics, psychology and sociology. There is where the holders-pressers debate rages.

Thus what it means to be an "evangelical" today is nowhere near as clear as it was even five years ago. So our definition of that term here must remain tentative, yet precise enough to give the evangelicals the unique identity they have earned.

My sources of information were widely varied. They include books, articles, and field research including interviews, attendance at evangelical gatherings including worship services, scholarly meetings, weekend retreats, adult forums and academic conventions. Some information on the movement is missing because those who could have furnished it did not respond to my inquiries.

Next, not every major group standing under the umbrella of "evangelical" between 1976 and 1980 is examined as fully as others. Missing here are extended discussions of Inter-Varsity Christian Fellowship, Campus Crusade, Oral Roberts, Rex Humbard, Young Life, and others. Those certainly helped the movement grow. They were, however, well established before 1976 and their contributions after that were more continuations of earlier priorities than they were innovative contributions to the current revival.[10] (I state that not as a criticism, but as a part of the historical record).

Some readers may wonder why the neo-Pentecostal movement is not included in this book. On close examination, I understand it to embrace a wider and more diverse collection of believers and traditions than those who have constituted the evangelical movement. Neo-Pentecostal is an ally, but not an organic member.

Regarding my method of organization, I need to explain two things. This work uses the case study method of specific trends within the revival rather than making a broad synthesis of all available evidence. Where possible, I attempted to use in some depth the contributions of one author, the person who made a major contribution to a given question. The case study is appropriate because it shows that among evangelicals in these years, much of the momentum for revival was indeed carried forward by individuals, including national celebrities, who by force of publicity as well as argument helped mold evangelical opinion.

Secondly, as to structure, this story falls quite logically into four parts: the historical background, the war among scholars over inerrancy and social issues; the expression of born again revivalism on the local, popular level of understanding, and the demonstration of cultural maturation by the smoothly orchestrated participation by evangelicals in the national political campaign of 1980. Granted that separation of the story into these parts, especially the scholarly from the popular expressions has not been absolute, I discovered that the various camps were far enough apart to warrant separate categories for analysis. The academy versus the marketplace cleavage (Part Two and Three below) is as old as our records of historical expression; today's revival shows no signs of this split being healed.

Finally, I have been mindful of a comment made by a book reviewer talking about another subject. He said, in effect, that simply because an historian "has accumulated a great deal of evidence and produces a narrative and analysis which seem plausible, that does not necessarily guarantee that the historian has proven anything."[11] The reviewer asks the historians to provide documentation rather than plausibility to convince the reader that his or her account is accurate. I hope the documentation I present, if not fully convincing to all readers, is more than plausible.

CHAPTER II

THE FORTUNES OF THE OLD-TIME RELIGION
1945-1960

Historians are often accused of being the first persons to
know when an era or age closes. The actors in the drama of history, those who create it, must wait until historians announce when
an epoch has been completed. As arbitrary as that may sound, we
continue to establish with certainty those turning points or signals
which inform us that a new day is here, an old one now past.

Such a new age surely appeared for Americans and all the
world in 1945, as momentous a single year perhaps as Western history has known. Only now are we realizing how deeply the events
of that time severed mankind's direct sense of continuity with his
past. Life in the post-World War II years was forced to come to
terms with an agenda with escalating terrors born out of the war
years. These included: the staggering tasks of feeding the throngs
of displaced refugees and somehow starting life over again with
millions of persons forever gone and cities and farms in ruins;
somehow absorbing some inkling of the enormity of the crime of the
Nazis against mankind in the holocaust of exterminating some six
million Jews and others; coming to recognize the perils of living
in a world in which radioactive atomic weapons could wipe out and
contaminate whole regions in a single detonation; coping with the
first, unmistakeable signs in the Third World that Western imperialism could not survive the determination of colonial nations to be

independent; pondering the likelihood that China would soon come
under Communist direction; and finally, fearing that in the flush
of victory over the Axis powers the Western nations would soon face
another threat to world stability in the early post-VJ Day advances
of the Soviet Union.

Obviously not all of these forces were as clearly understood
in 1945 as they would be some five years later. Americans in that
year were caught up in the joys of peace, the return home of the
G.I.s to a time a greater prosperity and opportunity than the nation had known for decades, and to bask in the knowledge that
their defeat of the Axis was the work of God. Once again America
had proved it could carry out the task God had given it to preserve freedom and liberty for the world. The two-way convenant
was still intact; as long as **America** did God's work on earth, He
would reward it with the blessings of peace and prosperity.

Yet, as Winston Churchill would later detect, such euphoria
was only an illusion. The West moved quickly from "Triumph to
Tragedy", as the title of his book for those years suggests. As the
1940s wore on, the crises of the new era increased in severity. Observers on both sides of the Atlantic talked increasingly of the
new age as being dominated not only by major economic and political dilemmas, but since the Soviet ideology was consciously anti-
religious, at rockbed the world was being gripped by a spiritual
conflict of the deepest order. So severe were the problems that they
required not only carefully planned social and economic solutions,
but the willpower to find the spiritual resources to attempt to even
try to solve them at all.

Significantly, one of those who would later become a pivotal
figure in reforming the evangelical tradition of post-war America,
Carl F.H. Henry, then a young professor at a Baptist seminary near
Chicago, diagnosed the global crises in prophetic terms. He found
signs of death erupting everywhere; in the smoldering cities, the
slaughtered populaces, the homeless and starving, and in the determination of the world's superpowers to strengthen their own interests at the expense of world harmony. Henry wrote that unless

a sweeping restoration of conservative Christianity was achieved rapidly, "humanity itself would not long survive the ruins of its dying culture...." Only a complete turning to accept the grace of God as channeled through the churches could rescue America and, over time, the world. Mankind could not solve its problems by itself; whatever solutions existed would come only from a revival to know and do God's will on earth.[1]

The theme of revival found little support, however, in the late 1940s. Signs of some growing interest in religious life did appear, including increased church membership and enrollment in college religion courses. Henry's call, however, remained only that; the times were not yet ripe.

As the decade moved toward its close, the sudden appearance of several apparently related events centering on foreign policy and alleged domestic espionage captured the headlines for several months. News commentators and political leaders alike detected a massive conspiracy of Communists at work to advance their influence through the world and infiltrate high government positions at home. Americans worried deeply over charges being made that spies for the Soviets had given Russia secrets for the atomic bomb; and the government produced the Rosenbergs, Alger Hiss, and others as proof such espionage did exist. Political office seekers demanded to know why China, after being supported so strongly by America, fell to the Communists; why North Korea was able to invade its south, and why in 1949 the Soviets were able to detonate their own atomic bomb. Surely, the consensus went, something more than coincidence was at work here. Was it not possible Communists were ready to seize America?

Given such an atmosphere, it was not surprising that revivalism should break out. Its first major breakthrough appeared in Los Angeles, headed during a sawdust trail revival by a young preacher, Billy Graham. With some experience in altar call preaching, but with no national recognition at the time, Graham's crusades starting in September, attracted little attention. Then one

evening, and as it turned out, the most important evening of his
career, Graham preached on the threats of Communist aggression
for America. Insisting that Soviet triumphs were a judgment by God
on America's failure to repent and turn to Him in revival, Graham
caught the listener's full attention with the statement that Communists "are more rampant in Los Angeles than any other city in
America. We need a revival." Unless that occurred, Graham pre-
dicted the enemy would drop three atomic bombs; one on New York,
one on Chicago, and one on Los Angeles. [2]

That pronouncement propelled Graham for the first time on to
the nation's front pages. Apparently, one of the housemaids at the
home of the enormously influential journalist, William Randolph
Hearst, Jr., heard Graham's sermon and told her employer about
it. Within hours Hearst sent his newspapers a telegram, "Puff
Graham"; that is, give his revival full publicity. The news coming
a few days later that some media celebrities had come forward at
Graham's altar call convinced another giant of American journalism,
Henry R. Luce of Time-Life that here indeed was a newsmaker, perhaps a prophet. As did Hearst, Luce gave Graham's crusade extended publicity, complete with photographs and commentary. Within
a few weeks, the preacher, son of a North Carolina dairy farmer,
was a nationally famous crusader. The revival Henry had called
for started to roll.

Graham quickly attracted large crowds, much earlier than any
earlier revival, as he preached across the country. He continued
his emphasis on Communism as a moral judgment on America; to
that, he added condemnations of materialism, moral laxity and spiritual indifference as sweeping over America. His success enabled
his staff to expand their publicity and long range planning. Soon
Graham found himself booked for as many as two years in advance.
During the waiting months, men from his office made the necessary
arrangements in cities selected for a Graham crusade.

Graham's success could be traced in part to his message, and
in part to his efficient promotion. Beyond that, he had an extraordinary appeal because of his simple, direct message and because

he himself seemed proof that despite its many internal weaknesses, America was still strong and good enough to produce so wholesome a warrior for the Lord as was Billy Graham. Since those in the national government had not found the means to turn back the Communist advance, revivalists argued, then perhaps Americans should get on their knees and repent, turning wholly to God for survival, perhaps even victory over atheistic Communism. Graham's presence, in brief, found a warm and large audience during the early and dark years of American conflict with the Soviets.

As the 1950s emerged, convincing new evidence pointed to the fact that the nation might well be on the brink of a full-scale revival. Tens, perhaps hundreds of thousands of Americans, strongly supported the preaching and writing of another national figure, Dr. Norman Vincent Peale. Basing his message on the benefits to be reaped by "positive thinking", Peale told his audience they could preserve their freedom, resist Communism, prosper in their work, and stay happy in their personal lives by formulating and keeping on repeating uplifting, positive thoughts. One such cluster of reinforcers for believers was to "think big, believe big, act big, pray big." From his church in New York City, Peale created a national network of influence through radio, newspaper columns, books, and his own magazine all of which told worried Americans that God was on their side, preserving free enterprise capitalism, the blessings of the work ethic, and emotional good health.[3]

So too, on the popular level of religious understanding, there emerged the Roman Catholic counterpart of Peale in the magnetic television presence and preaching of Bishop Fulton Sheen. He captivated viewers just getting acquainted with the magic of the silver screen at home, with a message of peace of mind. The mass market quickly absorbed songs such as "He" or "The Man Upstairs." C.B. DeMille filled cinema theaters with epocal, refurbished Bible stories.

On another level, substantial fresh interest in the study of theology appeared in colleges and universities. Major religious thinkers, such as the brothers H. Richard and Reinhold Niebuhr, and Paul Tillich, and Europeans such as Karl Barth and Emil Brunner received a far more respectful hearing than earlier writers. Within organized religious life, it became clear church membership, weekly attendance at services, financial support and new church construction were all clearly increasing with impressive speed. Observers and critics alike agreed; some kind of revival was at hand.

Yet this resurgence was fragmented, reflecting accurately the wide range of religious styles and forms of expression so characteristic of American religious life. By comparison to earlier crusades, this one lacked, in its early years, any clearly recognized leadership or a widely agreed upon agenda of concerns. Into this vacuum stepped Graham and Henry (longtime personal friends from their time together in Chicago), along with clerical and business friends to launch in 1956 a major new program to give direction and substance to the revival. They announced in that year the beginning of a journal, named Christianity Today to meet the need for a responsible, non-denominational journal. This would bring the best of evangelical thought and information to the public which, the journal's founders knew, too often regarded evangelical revivalists as fanatics or moneygrubbers.

In their statement of purpose and belief, the editors committed the journal to advancing what they believed to be the irrespressible surge of evangelical Christianity now taking shape across the country. They understood Christianity Today, along with the preaching crusades of Graham which they enthusiastically endorsed, as the spearheads of this newly refurbished expression of old-time evangelical revivalism; that movement now had concrete expression in the religious marketplace. The editors stated that the journal would uphold the Bible as "the authoritative disclosures of God's word and purpose and thus it is the rule of faith and life...." They made eight doctrinal affirmations, all harmonious with conservative, Reformed Protestantism.[4] Graham contributed an article to this first issue, stating that evangelicals understood the Bible as the inerrant, authoritative, verbally inspired word of God. Graham called on evangelicals and those searching for "authority, finality, and conclusiveness" in their faith to support the magazine. Prof. Henry was named as editor-in-chief. Considerable financial support came from invited businessmen, the most substantial being an on-going grant from J. Howard Pew of Sun Oil Company.   Virtually every ordained Protestant minister in the nation received a free subscription to it.

Somewhere in the early 1950s Graham, Henry, and other evan-gelical leaders started exploring the possibility of building on their growing support to give the movement the leadership and clear focus of an old time, traditional revival. Their successes so far convinced them God had given them a signal to rescue America and, in time, the world--the theme Henry had called up in 1946. Where else but in New York City, considered by evangelicals as "Babylon-on-the-Hudson," the city Graham had called America's most sinful, for a full-scale crusade. From there, God willing, it could spread across the nation as the earlier great revivals of the nation had done. Aware that earlier revivalists had considered New York as a "graveyard for evangelicals", and alert to the extensive media preparations demanded by such a campaign, Graham, Henry and the others committed themselves to this kind of revival in the belief that God could work a great miracle there.[5]

After months of extensive and energetic planning, the Billy Graham Evangelistic Crusade announced the revival would start in Madison Square Garden on May 15, 1957. The directors had left little planning undone, utilizing fully the most current media equipment and promotional advertising. They hoped that somehow this crusade would not be limited, as were Graham's earlier ones, to revival in just one specific city or region. This crusade might well envelop the nation. The Graham team and supporting evangeli-cal leaders were willing to commit themselves to turning America to God by means of a traditional holding fast which to them was true revival.

In New York Graham and his team carried out the same format for crusade programs they had developed over the last seven years;

a union choir, vocal solos, brief testimonials by well known converts, the Graham sermon, altar call, counselling for those who
came forward, and the benediction. Large numbers of seekers came
from out-of-state locations, usually on planned chartered buses or
trains. All of this, plus Graham's frequent appearances to smaller
groups in the city, received the full major-league kind of media
coverage that was the specialty of New York journalism. Graham
also received sharp criticism, as well as fulsome praise, from the
media which soon came to consider the crusade as one more entertainment event.

Having planned at first to stay one month, the Crusade leadership was surprised and grateful that the crowds after the initial
curiosity wore off, continued to hold their own, and even to increase. The leaders looked through the evidence for the sign they
wanted most to find: that the revival was spreading out from
Manhattan to neighboring states, and even beyond. Graham himself
expanded the scope of the Crusade's direct concern by starting to
emphasize that the revival aimed not only at saving New York, but
indeed at saving America, imperiled as it was by spiritual indifference. Early accounts sent to the Crusade leaders talked of substantial increase in weekly congregational services in the area,
of marked renewal of interest in evangelical preaching and witnessing and, of course, the nightly tally of those who had come
forward at the altar call. For a few brief weeks, as the leaders
decided to extend the crusade through the summer months, they believed an old-time revival was imminent. With such assurance they
found no reason to shift their emphasis from holding fast to that
of pressing on. The highest priority throughout the summer continued to be the call for individual repentance based on loyalty
to traditional doctrine. Despite its use of the most up-to-date technology, the continuity of this revival with the past remained intact.

Yet even at this moment of apparent victory, signs of slow-
down and indifference started reaching Crusade headquarters. These
were more than the expected indications of resistance to ongoing

growth. Despite a flurry of enthusiasm for the Labor Day finale, observers and friends alike realized the revival was not going national. Indeed, shortly after it left New York, it seemed the revival had never occurred there. When the post-mortems started to appear in substantial numbers, the analysists came forward with several explanations. Some thought Graham had made conversion and the introduction to the Christian life too easy; others pointed to a lack of effective follow-up by local congregations to the converts. Some believed the congregations who hopefully would nurture the new believers chose rather to remain centers for community activity rather than springboards for fresh evangelism.

Perhaps the best brief summation of it all came in an editorial in Christianity Today. Acknowledging that powerful social and economic changes had occurred in recent years, the editors stated, "an enormous increase in pure selfishness..." could not be easily detected but was at the heart of the resistance to revival. Where once, in a more golden past, Americans had been friendly and helpful, now they were preoccupied with upward financial mobility, demanding more leisure time, showing less interest in their jobs, and considering the highest good for themselves to be indulging in personal pursuits rather than evangelization and the improvement of society. To the editors, this trend was more rampant in America by the end of the 1950s than ever before.[6] The long hoped for revival of evangelical faith had won converts, it had made its testimony to America, but it had stopped right there.

CHAPTER III

THE 1960s: A FUNDAMENTAL SHIFT

Even as the revivalist stream of American religious life slowed
down, others were steadily building strength and form, ready to
spread across the nation. During the 1950s these had been as yet
tiny rivulets, stirring quietly under the glacier-like dominance of
the conservatism of those years. In the next decade they burst into
full public view, cascading into virtually every major area of
American life.

This rapid, unexpected relocation, by McLoughlin's definition
an "awakening", would shake the most cherished national institutions: family, church, government, schools, and business. None
went untouched. From this would emerge, in Sydney E. Ahlstrom's
estimate, "a fundamental shift in American moral and religious attitudes." The familiar terrain of "not only historical Western theism
but also the older forms of national confidence and social idealism
--not to mention traditional moral sanctions and standards of public
behavior"--were permanently altered.[1]

Evangelicals, by no means in retreat during the 1960s, would
find they needed new maps and instructions for survival. And survival was a worthy enough accomplishment for any tradition-rooted
institution in those years. To understand the evangelicals' response
to this awakening, we should first look at the shape and substance
(in summary form) of this fundamental shift.

Standing out as the most distinctive ingredients of the decade
were the related themes of protest and liberation; protest against

that which the new activists considered pernicious and destructive in American life, and liberation from such bondage opening an entrance into a land committed to peace and freedom. The protest movements, virtually invisible a decade earlier, now sprang up along a very wide spectrum; the Black revolution, women's liberation, ethnic pride groups, the collegiate Free Speech Movement, the ecological initiative, involvement of clergy in social protest and anti-draft and anti-war crusades. Each, in its own way, would demand that the nation's policies and institutions impeding liberation be altered as quickly and completely as possible. In the words of one of the slogans of the 60s: "What do we want? Freedom! When do we want it? Now!!!"

That word 'now' captures much of the inner meaning of the several protests. After centuries of being oppressed or ignored by the existing powers and attitudes and institutional indifference, the new activists decided that now they could, they must turn America into a free society. Any further delay would prove complicity with those who were defending the status quo. Hence no commitment was too strong, no expression of dedication too great when done in the name of one's cause. Rivulets became streams, some of which were irrepressible.

The demands for "now" suggest the depth of the protesters' commitment to their causes. Not willing to accept token concessions or piecemeal reforms, each crusade set its sights for permanent liberation. In visionary terms, they believed that once freed from the oppressive hand of the past they would know this country to again be the haven for the free. By liberation from past bondage, social role stereotyping, and exploitation they would achieve (in a favorite 60's term) "self actualization". They would be free to achieve authentic selfhood, celebrating their distinctiveness, unshackled by those who had degraded them through racial, economic or sexual bondage. One sympathetic observer called all this "the greeening of America", a time of spring, of hope, of new birth.

Yet millions of other Americans wanted to maintain the status quo. To them, given the name of "middle Americans", demands such as full equality for Blacks, women, Chicanos or native Americans must be resisted. In another realm, college officials yielded as little ground as possible to students demanding full control over their personal lives. Clergy active in the protest movements found themselves less than popular with their congregations or superiors. The environmentalist groups discovered how powerful the established business interests were in blocking their call for protecting the ecology of the natural world.

To holders fast, the protest movements demanded reforms which simply were contrary to God's will. Had not the nuclear family evolved over the centuries as an ideal approximation of Christians being one family under God? Were not both black and white really the happiest when each stayed with their own? Would not higher education proceed ahead with its major mission most effectively when the division of power on campuses was explicit and enforced? Would not loyalty to this nation be destroyed by continuing anti-draft and anti-war crusades? Would not the rights of private property be wiped out by making concessions to environmentalists who had no personal or stockholder investments at stake? No, holders fast argued, institutions existed as they stood for a reason. Radical change would produce not peace and freedom, but would inevitably lead to anarchy.

The middle Americans had little trouble in the 60s locating the enemy. In a wide variety of ways, the protesters started their several protests against the standpatters. Most visibly (and audibly, with rock music) they formed a very loose but vivid "counterculture" centering around non-traditional hair and clothes styles, devotion to rock music, and a disdain of middle American commitment to neatness, cleanliness, and order. The counterculture was an extraordinary blending, mostly of people between 16 and 30, of pacifists, vegetarians, feminists, civil righters, dropouts, and assorted nonconformists brought together by "the unity of what they were rebelling against."[2]

These "hippies" as friends and critics labelled them, stood out as frightening evidence to middle Americans of what lay in store if such protesters ever gained power, or if their own children joined the movement. To them, America had become great by its fidelity to traditional norms of order and decency; this was no time to let those triumphs be destroyed.

No one obviously had planned this awakening, no master plan was being circulated among the protesters. In retrospect, it seems the first tangible signs emerged in 1960 when Black students staged the first sit-in protest at a Greensboro, North Carolina, segregated lunch counter. Then in increasing numbers came more civil rights protesters, "Freedom Riders" of blacks and whites seeking to integrate public facilities. In 1963 Betty Friedan brought out The Feminine Mystique, accepted now as the first major statement of the new women's movement. A year later the Free Speech Movement by students at University of California, Berkeley, demanded greater student autonomy. Congress set about looking carefully at reform legislation.

Despite some signs of progress, such as the Civil Rights acts of 1964 and 1965, the demands for change and the backlash against those demands continued to mount in mid-decade. Black ghettoes in Watts, Detroit, Newark, and elsewhere erupted into civil war between the populace and the police; campuses such as Cornell, Yale, Wisconsin-Madison and Harvard among others became battlegrounds for fixed combat between militant activists and law enforcement agencies. Then came the first reports of increased American military action in Vietnam, the weekly announcement from the Pentagon on American casualties there, and television news stories showing U.S. Marines burning villages populated only by civilians. Fanning the discontent among the voters were political office seekers demanding that all this protest be stopped and America restored to its rightful role of stability and loyalty. The nation by 1968 was perilously divided. [3]

Strained as it had been before that year, American society became something of a nightmare in 1968. The great unifier of the

civil rights movement, Martin Luther King, Jr., was assassinated
in April. Those young adults protesting against the war but wanting to work within the boundaries of the political system, found
themselves bereft when in June their candidate for the Presidency,
Senator Robert F. Kennedy, was murdered. The women's movement
met with a well organized, militant blacklash from, of all things,
other women. And the war continued to escalate, and campus riots
grew into events such as the two nights of terror and death at
Columbia University in the wake of a riotous student protest.

The nation's attention turned to the coming Democratic National Convention, scheduled for August in Chicago. There, the protesters believed, they had at least a chance to use the party and
the coming Presidential campaign for their crusades: ending the
draft and the war, extending equality to the minorities, the Equal
Rights Amendment, curbing pollution--the whole gamut of issues of
the day. To that city came a full assortment of dissenters and crusaders; the counterculture, Black and women's caucuses, and an
embittered group of combat veterans from Vietnam all of whom
wanted to stop American involvement there, even if that meant
America would have to admit military defeat for the first time in
its history.

The disasters that occurred outside the convention hall (and
the shenanigans taking place within) are such familiar history that
they need not be repeated here.[4] None of the authority or prestige
of such institutions as a national political party, the police, the
National Guard or involved clergy working among the dissenters
could prevent the outbreak of violence as demonstraters and police
clashed throughout the downtown. Order was restored only when (as
the official study of events explained) the Chicago police went on
a riot of physical repression. They used unrestrained force to hold
back the street demonstrators from trashing downtown stores, invad-
ing the Convention hotels, and marching to the Convention center
several miles south of the Loop. So brutal was the police reaction
to the often mindless and unlawful provocations of the demonstrators that it brought the Convention delegates to realize how close

to chaos they all stood. Somehow the convention ended, the demonstrators were released from jail and left town. But the nation and,
as the protesters changed, "the whole world" was watching.

Throughout the mounting series of crises during the decade,
the evangelicals stood publically united against all but the most
moderate reformist demands for liberation in its many forms. Accus-
tomed more as they were to concentrating on evangelism aimed at
winning individual conversions than speaking on national issues,
they saw the events of the 60s as further evidence of how much
America needed to repent and restore the traditional values they
espoused.

Yet they concluded the times were not well suited for launching a national revival. Rather the leading spokesmen gave increasing attention to the major protest movements.[5] On civil rights they
generally counselled a moderate course of working for improving
the attitudes of individual Blacks and whites towards each other
rather than support national legislation such as the Civil Rights
acts of 1964 and 1965 as being too coercive and moving towards integration too rapidly. On women's rights, they agreed that in principle women deserved equal treatment, but they saw grave dangers
to the stability of the nuclear family were women to consider ca-
reers more important than their God-given duties as wives and
mothers. They, with most of the rest of the citizenry, sharply criticized the violence erupting on the campuses. They supported
equally the principle of greater protection of the natural environment but again expressed worries that national government solutions
would be too coercive and endanger the rights of property owners.[6]

As the decade moved ahead, the evangelicals realized the most
serious dilemma was that of the nation dividing over American intervention in Vietnam. They concluded that much of the public's
confusion and polarization resulted from the fact that everyone expected this to be a war fought by traditional means such as large
scale battles. Yet such was not the case; when no major victories
could be announced or new sustained offensives taken or direct

threats to America's domestic security from the North Vietnamese indicated, the public grew perplexed over what kind of a war it really was. In this situation, the evangelical spokesmen said, the citizens must trust the government's policies in conducting the war. Washington had the information, it probably was carrying on secret peace negotiations and it was the duty of the people to support their government in time of war. As a result, the Christianity Today editors showed more irritation in 1965 over the growing number of clergy and laity from National Council of Churches organizations demonstrating against the war than they did in the military escalation ordered by President Lyndon Johnson. They also sharply criticized the "ten to fifteen thousand students" who had "left campus and books behind to tell President Johnson what to do about Vietnam. One wonders how undergraduates get so smart so soon."[7]

In 1966 the evangelicals printed an article highly revealing of their reactions to the war, contributed by General William K. Harrison, entitled "Is the United States Right in Bombing North Vietnam?" Harrison answered the question in the affirmative, arguing that the effort to defeat decisively the military aggression of the Communists in South Vietnam was a part of the Christian's eternal battle against evil. The author reminded the audience that "there can be no peace until the Prince of Peace comes at the Second Advent." "Apart from God's intervention there can be no lasting peace." Harrison concluded that only the Great Tribulation would bring an end to war. He called on Christians "to look to God in faith for guidance and wisdom for their government and for themselves, that they may follow a path of integrity and justice, seeking peace, but not afraid to fight if necessary, and withal not hating their enemies."[8]

Harrison's reference to the "Great Tribulation" reflected a loyalty to evangelistic acceptance of how the End Times would come to this world. This terminology taught that war was inevitable; that as in II Timothy 3:1, "in the last days perilous times shall come." As the level of violent protest over the war, racism, sexism, and campus issues escalated during the late 60s the leaders

talked with greater frequency that such signs indicated the final
days of this planet were now upon the world; the Great Tribulation
and Armageddon were indeed imminent. Under such conditions, these
writers continued, men delude themselves by thinking they could
attain "world peace". Only personal conversion and revival of commitment to Christ could suffice in these last days.[9]

Yet as the war continued, some evangelicals slowly but clearly started to reconsider their position. For one thing, the evangelical Senator Mark Hatfield was calling for rapid disengagement. And
in the late 60s the most influential leader of all, Billy Graham,
gradually moved from an all out hawk position to one of anguish
over the failure to achieve victory and the dangers of national division. Graham had consistently preached, as he said in every sermon, that "The Bible says..." or states a specific Christian stance
on the great issues of the times. Throughout his public career he
had interpreted Communist foreign policy as a tool used by Satan
to convert the world to atheism. When in 1965 several peace groups
called on Johnson to end the war, Graham responded in a nationally
broadcast sermon with a sermon "When Silence is Yellow." He asked
Americans to emulate Martin Luther at the Diet of Worms to "speak
out" without being afraid of being called "controversial" or upset-
ting the status quo. Graham wanted Americans to "add the weight
of our names to some ideals, convictions, and beliefs." He concluded:

> We have our peace movements, and all we want is peace
> --abroad and at home. But if by peace we mean ap-
> peasing tyranny, compromising with gangsters and be-
> ing silent because we haven't the moral fortitude to
> speak out against injustice, then this is not real peace.
> It is a false peace. It is a farce and a hoax.

In his ending he pointed out that a nation that would not fight
for its freedom could not "long endure. When a people have lost
their ideals and have stopped fighting for them, their country is
doomed." [10]

In 1966 at Johnson's request Graham spent the Christmas season visiting American military personnel in Vietnam. He stated that "millions of Americans are very proud of you. Their prayers and hopes are with you. God bless you." Two years later he made the same trip, repeating that he brought greetings from millions of Americans "who are proud of you and what you are doing."[11]

When asked by reporters whether the United States should step up military involvement or start scaling them down, Graham said he left the military direction of the war to the President and that he "wasn't entering the hawk or dove side of the war. I've not even taken a position on whether we should be in Vietnam." When Graham mentioned this stand to President Johnson the latter replied, "All right, Billy. When those newspaper guys get you in a corner, just tell them you're a friend of the President of the United States and he'll go anywhere in the world for peace." Graham later told a New York reporter that early in the war he had favored an all-out military effort, or no effort at all, but by 1969 he had reconsidered and believed then that the war was "over-Americanized." His trips to the troops there were a part of his spiritual ministry which, he believed, did not compromise his stand on neutrality.[12]

At the same time Graham was warning that the anti-war protests "so exaggerate our divisions over the war that they could make Hanoi confident it will eventually win." Some months later he expressed his hope that the war would soon end because the by-products of the conflict were creating very serious conflicts within the nation. It had "opened the way for extremists to seize upon the flag and traditional American values and make them their own. We have allowed the world 'patriotism' to get into the hands of some right wingers." He admitted: "I don't guess anybody loves the flag more than some of the people that are against the war."[13]

The question Graham did not answer directly in his public statement was whether the Bible said what was right or wrong about American military involvement in Vietnam. He had stayed aloof with the comment that the President was in charge of military operations, but repeatedly he and other evangelicals had stated their opinions on issues other than the military over which the President also had charge. Only on the most crucial national question of the day did Graham remain neutral. That stance, however, should not be considered unusual nor vacillating. It reflected the national dilemma created by the war; the Bible taught God's will for man on every problem he faced but it did not (or could not) unite the nation at this point.

During these latter years of the 60s, due largely to the increased disputes among evangelicals over the war, the first tiny but measurable signs of conflict appeared between holders fast and pressers on. Graham's position on the war is one such instance. Few pressers on were evident at that time, but more significantly the leading holders fast showed signs of admitting their position was not altogether sound. The evangelicals realized they could not stand as a single voice by simply making one more round of condemnation against the liberals and radicals. Carl F. H. Henry squarely faced this issue in 1968 by acknowledging that many of the criticisms by the younger adults about the crisis in American life were well taken. He had by then detected unmistakeable signs that the younger evangelicals were impatient with the holders' fast demands for loyalty to the old tradition for loyalty's sake, with their impatience with the "do not" code of ethics by the older generation, by their distrust of those adults who were hung up on such incidentals as hair and dress styles rather than telling the Good News of the gospel. Henry concluded that "evangelicals are not winning the younger generation any more than deviant and distorted forms of Christianity are." He and the editors of Christianity Today deplored the growing polarization between generations; "seldom has evangelical Christianity faced larger opportunities in America, and seldom has its leadership been more needed."[14]

The first measurable signs that some kind of pressers on movement was emerging came from the writings of an energetic, well educated group of intellectuals within the tradition; their prime

concern was increasing social involvement of the evangelicals. They
wanted fresh ideas and concrete proposals from the seminaries, colleges, pulpits, and journals to help end the war, heal racial and
sexual oppression, ameliorating the poverty crunch for the disad-
vantaged, for a more responsible position on population control,
and for a recognition that the "welfare state" was not necessarily
the handiwork of Satan. They found inspiration and leadership for
their proposals in the legislative records of two prominent lawmakers, Senator Mark Hatfield and Congressman John B. Anderson.
Serious as the gap was, Henry suggested that it was wide but not
impossible to bridge so long as all evangelicals remained loyal
to "the inscripturated truths of the inerrant Bible" and "evangelical
rational theism."[15] His hopes for unity would turn out to be something less successful than he was here predicting.

CHAPTER IV

Years of Distress, 1968-1974

The awakening of the 1960s contained such power that it touched every American. By 1968 the citizens realized its momentum was transforming the very quality of their lives. The pressures for both change and for standing pat had become so strong they strained the capacity of the major social governing institutions of the day to limits rarely known before in American history. Even the flag itself became a symbol of the clash. The radicals used it as clothing, for curtains, and in other non-traditional ways. The middle Americans responded with flag decals for their cars, flag lapel buttons and sleeve patches. What would transpire in the years 1968-74 would be the result of that awakening, especially as it reshaped the yet embryonic evangelical response by the pressers on.

To this point, as we have seen, they constituted only a minute portion of the evangelical camp. The overwhelming majority of the larger group believed that if the governing institutions would succumb and adapt to what they perceived the counterculture's alternatives to be, then America would be destroyed. Nowhere was their sentiment better summarized than in an immensely popular essay by Alan Macintosh of Luverne, an editor of a Minnesota weekly newspaper. Entitled "I Am a Tired American," it said:

> I am a tired American...tired of having the world pan-
> handlers use my country as a whipping boy...weary of
> having American embassies stoned, burned, and sacked
> ...fed up with mobs of long-haired youths who claim

they represent the 'new wave' of America and sneer at
the old-fashioned virtues of honesty, integrity, and morality...nauseated by the lazy do-nothings who wouldn't
take a job if you drove them to work in a Rolls Royce
...getting madder by the minute at the filth-peddlers
who have launched America on an obsenity race...
angered by the self-righteous breast beater critics of
America.[1]

Needing to believe that a viable solution could be found, middle Americans responded enthusiastically to the Presidential campaign oratory of Republican candidates Richard M. Nixon and Spiro
Agnew. In his nomination acceptance speech Nixon captured the essence of their frustrations and their hopes. He acknowledged that
many (obviously the Blacks and the poor) wanted success but found
only "a nightmare of poverty and neglect and despair." But the
dream for a better life persisted, embodied in his own "journey
through life." By the aid of self-sacrificing parents, great teachers, inspirational ministers, a courageous wife, and a loyal public
who "stood by him in victory and defeat," he now stood before the
nation "nominated for the President of the United States.... For
most of us," he assessed accurately, "the American dream has come
true. And what I ask you to do tonight is to help me make that
dream come true for millions to whom it's an impossible dream today."[2] Although not organized in any way as a voter bloc, large
numbers of evangelicals were among the citizens who elected the
Republican ticket by the narrowest of margins over Senators Hum-
phrey and Muskie. Graham himself had lent his full prestige to the
Republican cause by being among Nixon's advisors suggesting names
for the Vice-Presidential running mate (he had suggested Mark Hatfield). Nixon reciprocated by speaking, in May of 1970, at a Graham revivalist service in Knoxville, the first President to speak
at such a gathering. Nixon later involved Graham in two diplomatic
missions, briefing him privately about his planned trip to Communist China and having him serve as the Presidential representative
at the inauguration of Dr. William Tolbert as President of Liberia.[3]

Very much the spokesman for the holders fast, Graham in 1969 preached that permanent peace was an illusion; permanent peace would come only with the Second Coming. He called on Americans to reject what he believed were the liberals' belief that economic solutions would meet mankind's spiritual needs or that democracy could survive without a religious faith. He called for "a renewal of faith in God, faith in one another, faith in America, faith in everything our country is supposed to stand for."[4]

The prominence of Graham for the holders fast, pressers on controversy at this point in time becomes decisive, hence the detailed discussion given it here. Pressers on would react bitterly not only to his friendship with the incumbent President but at Graham's powerful leadership in a gala, highly publicized "Honor America Day" ceremony in Washington, DC on July 4, 1970. After several months of planning with the presidents of Reader's Digest Marriott Inns and other celebrities such as Walt Disney spokesmen and Bob Hope, Graham endorsed plans for a massive rally to tell everyone "we believe in the institutions of America."

Graham found six reasons to honor America; it had "opened her heart and her doors to the distressed and the persecuted of the world"; it had been "the most generous nation in history" ... sharing "our wealth and faith with a world in need"; it had "never hidden her problems"; America was "honestly recognizing and is courageously trying to solve her social problems"; "she defends the right of her citizens to dissent"; and finally "because there is woven into the warp and woof of our nation faith in God. The ethical and moral principles of the Judeo-Christian faith, and the God of that tradition are found in the Declaration of Independence." He called on Americans to "sing again! America needs to celebrate again! America needs to wave the flag again!" "Proudly gather around the flag and all that it stands for."[5]

One year later the first documentable protest not only against Graham but against the entire holders fast position by dedicated evangelicals would appear. They could not accept Nixon's (and by implication, Graham's) continuing the war in Vietnam, the invasion

of Cambodia, the mounting casualty lists, the cavalier treatment
the President showed his steadily increasing number of critics, and
the continuing economic and social plight of the oppressed. A group
of students at Trinity Evangelical Divinity School, Deerfield (near
Chicago) dedicated themselves to "Christian radicalism", a position
which meets the definition of "pressers on" defined above (pp. 5-6).
They published a bimonthly newspaper, carefully named "The Post-
American" (later to be Sojourners, see below, p. 67) searching
to connect the demands of evangelical faith with the public issues
of the day. One editor stated the purpose:

> We see our main industry as articulating a radical
> Christian response to war and injustice, and as orga-
> nizing groups and individuals committed to this into a
> network for prophetic action in America. As far as we
> can tell, we are the most organized and aggressive
> group with this understanding of the gospel east of the
> Rockies, but we are not interested in a strong organi-
> zation at all. Our hope lies in the moral awakening of
> the evangelical community....[6]

They quickly made known their disappointment with Graham
and the holders fast. They rejected his central priority that social
reform cannot take place before personal conversion; that the reborn
person would inevitably bring about an improved society. They rejected Graham's zestful linkage to American civil religion, America
as God's will and way as guardian of liberty and freedom for the
other nations of the world to follow. In 1972 The Post-American
editors directly responded to "Honor America". They wrote that in
each of the six reasons cited by Graham for waving flags, the historical record showed something else. Instead of opening her gates,
they pointed to the exploitation of ethnic minorities; instead of being genorous and sharing, America had supported the military dic-
tators of the world who suppressed the programs of their own poor;
they rejected America as never hiding its problems by pointing to
Nixon's attempted squelching of Daniel Ellsberg who published the

Pentagon Papers; instead of America recognizing and solving her social problems, the editors showed that sixty percent of the federal budget went to military programs; on the right to dissent, they pointed to the overpowering of students at Kent State and Chicago in 1968 and other places; and finally they could not believe that America was a nation under God because "Graham fails to distinguish between the God of American civil religion and the God of Judeo-Christianity." [7]

Their rebuttal is worth quoting at length as a pressers on position:

> Our God is the God of Abraham, Moses, Peter and Paul
> --not Jefferson, Washington, Johnson and Nixon. Our
> values are predicated upon the transcendent norms of
> a loving father who has revealed Himself in Jesus
> Christ--not an austere Provider of Blessings who gives
> a religious dimension to the developing American experi-
> ence. A commitment to our God demands prophetic judg-
> ment upon a corrupt and sinful society and a life-style
> consistent with His transcendent norms--not passive sub-
> mission to the State everytime it uses religious langu-
> age, motifs and symbols to justify American expan-
> ism. [8]

Under the Nixon administration, most of the energy behind the activism of the 60's agenda for America slowly slid back downhill. The war went on, the dissenters found themselves investigated by the F.B.I., they had no legislative victories from Congress to celebrate. Yet the full impact of recent years had not been lost on those now standing at the starting line of the pressers on camp. Momentum for change in American religious life has often been born at its think tanks, the seminaries, and then with rippled effect spread over the nation. The first ripple--causing stones for pressing on appeared now at not only Trinity but a landmark bastion of holding fast, Fuller Theological Seminary of Pasadena. Espousing fully traditional evangelical teachings, it encouraged full and free discussion from all standpoints of major ethical issues; it encouraged

study of the best of ecumenical and liberal theology, and allowed
the historical-critical method of Biblical text studies to be considered as a responsible option to familiar evangelical hermeneutics. Within a few years several other evangelical seminaries made
similar changes in their curriculum and campus life. [9]

Perhaps more concretely, the next significant step ahead for
pressers on turned up during the 1972 Presidential election. A small
but enthusiastic group organized an "Evangelicals for McGovern"
offensive. Rarely since the days of William Jennings Bryan (one of
America's political evangelicals par excellence) had evangelicals
so directly identified themselves with a presidential candidate.
In 1972 the leaders announced they could no longer condone what
they perceived as President Nixon's lack of concern for the Blacks
and the poor, the inequities in tax laws, and most of all, the con-
tinuation of the war.   They were impressed by Senator George
McGovern as a "peace candidate" and one who knew his Bible (he
was a preacher's son). The Board in the group included the Rev.
Walden Howard, editor of Faith at Work, evangelist Tom Skinner,
author and teacher Ron Sider, and professors in several fields from
such stalwart evangelical centers as Fuller, Wheaton Seminary,
Gordon College, Calvin College, Gordon-Conwell Seminary, Eastern
Baptist College, Bethel College, and editors of various evangelical
journals. [10]

Yet Nixon won easily, in fact overwhelmingly. Analysts such
as Seymour Martin Lipset and Earl Raab explained the outcome by
suggesting many, including evangelicals, voted against McGovern
because he was perceived as soft on the counterculture, on abortion
on demand, welfare, amnesty for draft evaders, marijuana, increasing government spending, and inflation. Those were not the kinds
of trends and issues the rank and file evangelicals wanted to see
extended into the next four years. [11] Yet evangelicals no longer
stood as a predictable voter bloc, a fact which Governor Jimmy
Carter of Georgia did not overlook four years later.

Throughout this the holders fast continued to hold center
stage.   Three major evangelistic programs, Explo 72, Key 73, and

the 1974 Lausanne Congress on World Evangelism in a united form each contributed to the evangelical's determination to keep alive the initiative and power of their convictions. Explo 72 was the creation of Campus Crusade for Christ, a parachurch campus ministry founded and directed by Bill Bright in 1950 and is today a major evangelical voice. Its directors concluded that now at the height of popularity of the youth-oriented Jesus revival young people should conduct "gigantic and never-to-be forgotten demonstration of God's love."

Billy Graham, Honorary Chairman, called on the some 80,000 in attendance at a Dallas stadium to dramatize that revival, witness for Christ, to remember "that the old-time Gospel is relevant to this modern generation"; to apply that faith to the day's crises, to muster new support for missionary work and "to say to the whole world that Christian youth are on the march."[12] To outside observers the crusade reflected how clearly its planners had realized the attractiveness of some aspects of counterculture lifestyles (rock groups, hippie style clothing and celebrities abounded) and how necessary the energy from that culture must be channelled into familiar expressions and affirmations. Small group seminars and plenary audiences examined not only the old-time Gospel but racism, war and the cost of discipleship, topics rarely voiced only a few years ago. The finale included a mass, standing altar call response in dedication to Christ to help evangelize the world. To hold fast, the youth must be recruited, and Explo 72 offered them that opportunity. Some radical Christian young adults made their dissenting presence known, but the spotlight never left those who planned and carried out the rally.

The momentum for evangelism continued the next year with plans through "Key 73" originally planned by Christianity Today to present a coordinated campaign "aimed at confronting every person in North America more fully and forcefully with the Gospel of Jesus."[13] Drawing on some 200,000 congregations from 150 denominations, the participants throughout the first three quarters of that year presented a diversified number of campaigns to bring the

gospel to every person. The primary emphasis centered on personal
conversion, the traditional strength of the evangelical voice. Participants attempted to present a single voice on that theme, re-
straining from rethreshing the old doctrinal arguments which had
kept them apart, and demonstrating that in carrying out the Great
Commission of Matthew 28 they were united.

In its summation in September the editors of Christianity Today stated "that never before have so many Scriptures been distri-
buted, so many Christian tracts presented, and so many doors
knocked upon for the sake of the Gospel. Evangelical enterprises are
operating at record peaks. Christian faith is strikingly evident
from bumper stickers to jewelry. People on this continent are more
conscious of the person of Jesus Christ than at any other time in
history. [emphasis mine]   Revival fires may not yet have been ig-
nited, but the sparks certainly are flying."[14] Conceding that not
every person was confronted, that no spectacular turnabout was
evident, the mandate to evangelize had been carried out, the story
had been told. The holders fast remained in command.

Although a pressers on statement came forward in November
with "A Declaration of Social Concern" (see below, pp. 153-54) the
third major evangelical call to action unfolded in July, 1974, not
in the United States but in Lausanne, Switzerland, the International
Congress on World Evangelism. In part a reaction against the more
irenic World Council of Churches' alternative way of spreading the
faith, this meeting was designed by evangelical leaders to reaf-
firm "the Old-Time Gospel". Some 2,430 participants from 150 countries heard sermons, conducted Bible studies, and learned evangelistic techniques appropriate for evangelism in different parts
of the world. Few representatives from Third World countries did
attend; and the Congress was directed by American and European
leaders. Specific proposals for implementing the ideas were made,
resolutions passed (some of great importance as seen below in the
consideration of biblical inerrancy, pp. 45-59) and again another
demonstration of traditional evangelical unity had been made.[15]

These constituted the major thrust of the more familiar priorities within this family of the many families of the community of faith. An earlier, highly significant expression recognizing the legitimacy of pressers on had been made a half year earlier, "The Chicago Declaration." That meeting would in the immediate years ahead prove to be something of a preview of today's impasse between the two major camps of evangelicalism, hence it is worth discussing here in some detail.

Proposed first at Explo 72 by The Post-American leaders, evangelical spokesman, under the direction of Ron Sider, invited "evangelicals" from a wide variety of positions to see whether some common ground of principles for affirming a commitment to social reform issues could be made. Those, about fifty in all, who came to Chicago for such an exploration were representatives of the "peace churches", Black groups, propositional doctrine advocates, younger social activists nurtured in the awakening of the 60s and a few well known elder statesman. By no means was the deck stacked in any direction other than there being only a handful of women invited, a grievous poor judgment acknowledged later by the planners.

Chances for any acceptable consensus seemed dim after the first three presentations; one, a sharp attack on racism by William Pannell; two, a plea by Nancy Hardesty for the delegates to take seriously the demands of women; and finally, a call by John Howard Yoder for a straightforward statement on the question of the evils of war. The debates over both substance and style continued for two more days. When the final vote came, a few declined to sign it, one being Yoder (author of the landmark work, The Politics of Jesus) because "they believed it didn't say enough."[16]

What it did say in toto can be found in Appendix I. The signers confessed their failure to acknowledge the "complete claims of God on our lives." This had led to the horrendous evils of racism, abstention from political involvement by evangelicals, an indifference to the nations' materialism and injustice towards poor people everywhere, an idolatrous faith in making "the nation and its institutions of near-religious loyalty"; a "prideful domination" by men over women and "irresponsible passivity by women." The conclusion proclaimed "no new Gospel, but the Gospel of our Lord Jesus Christ who, through the power of the Holy Spirit, frees people from sin so that they might praise God through works of righteousness. By this declaration we endorse no political ideology or party, but call our nation's leaders and people to that righteousness which exalts a nation. We make this declaration in the biblical hope that Christ is coming to consummate the Kingdom and we accept his claim on our total discipleship till He comes."[17] The conference was concluded with a "pinch of salt" celebration. Each in attendance was given a small portion of salt to remind them that when the Great Commission was given, the disciples were sent out as "salt of the earth."

Out of that gathering came a new group, "Evangelicals for Social Action," including the original signers and others sympathetic to its call. Some meetings to implement its principles were held in the next three years but "little was actually accomplished at these gatherings."[18] Yet in all of the committee meetings, debates and resolutions, the evangelicals were searching for both shared principles and specific programs of implementation to take up a new initiative in the nation's life. Internal disagreement was as old as the tradition itself, but a careful reading of the proceedings and statements reveals a new ingredient; holding fast and pressing on were not simply "the two sides of the same coin" as the old, comfortable cliche would have it. Holders fast in essence insisted on personal conversion as the prime concern. Pressers on insisted that a far greater involvement by evangelicals in direct public action over the great issues was of equal importance; the two were simply inseparable. The lines had been drawn, now only awaiting the sparks of revival fire some two years later to create ignition.

To evangelicals, and to the nation's citizenry at large, the pressures for doing something about the growing crises of the nation continued to mount during these years. Just as the final troops came home from Vietnam and President Gerald Ford issued a full pardon for any wrongdoings Richard Nixon had committed in the Watergate scandal, fresh and highly explosive new problems came into view. Out of the 60's awakening came the Equal Rights Amendment for women, polarizing voters and legislators; the Supreme Court in 1973 cleared the grounds for increasing greatly the number of legal abortions; vigorous, often bitter debate continued over environmentalist reforms to protect the environment; signs of runaway inflation cropped up, and everyone seemed certain some kind of "sexual revolution" was in process (see pp. 67-79).

By direct contrast to the 60s, however, the mood of the nation turned into one of indifference towards the solution of these problems, or the appearance of highly structured, militant "one issue" pressure groups, demanding immediate national attention be given their particular cause, be it pro-life or pro-choice, constitutional limitations on legislative spending, strengthening or weakening public controls over natural resources, demands for full equality among all people regardless of sex, race or ethnic origin. What was unusual about the 70s compared to the earlier decade was the willingness to work only for one's own personal crusade, or to escape from the clamor altogether. This latter trend helped spawn the emerging "self help movement" based on the premises that since the great problems were out of control, that politicians were only crooks, that really nothing on a major scale could be done. One's only salvation was in improving her or his own mental well being --the favorite phrase being "get in touch with your feelings." Hundreds of self help, human potential, inward growth kinds of programs now mushroomed in popularity for any searching American. Since the world made no sense, then perhaps through self help one could gain a measure of understanding and control over one's own life. Since the major institutions--church, government, business, education--stood helpless, then at least you could save yourself.

How? As the leading best seller entitled it by <u>Looking Out for Number One</u>, or <u>Pulling Your Own Strings</u> or achieving <u>Power Through Success</u>.[19]

The transition from the activism of the 1960s to the inward search of the 70s illustrates something of the enormous changes which had occurred in American life since 1945. Although covering only a twenty year span, the transformations in every area of the nation's culture were beyond anyone's full understanding. So much of the past, for so many people, seemed gone and forgotten. Yet daily life did continue; no one (as in the 60s) talked now about internal civil war. America somehow seemed to be muddling through, badly but surviving. Perhaps, observers suggested, the coming celebration of America's Bicentennial in 1976 would be the now-missing spark to ignite confidence in the future. Other observers, far fewer in number, looked across the scene in search of signs pointing to a revival.

PART TWO

HARVEST OF STALEMATE: EVANGELICALS DIVIDED

1976-1980

CHAPTER V

THE INSTANT IMPASSE: EVANGELICALS AND INERRANCY

INTRODUCTION

Drawing on the argument made by Paul Tillich that "Religion is the substance of culture; Culture is the form of religion," Sydney E. Ahlstrom concludes that "no one age is more religious than any other, though some do experience far more excruciating demands for change and adjustment than others even dream of. What changes are the modalities of religions and the forms of organization and expression. We thus do well to recognize that the culture of a nation, which is to say its collective behavior, reflects its dominant ethical and religious impulses."[1] What became clear by the late 1970s was that the awakening of the previous decade had created "excruciating demands for change and adjustment" in American life. The change with which we are concerned here is the revival, (the media called it a "resurgence") of evangelical faith. A revival, defined by William McLoughlin as "The Protestant ritual (at first spontaneous, but, since 1830, routinized) in which charismatic evangelists convey 'The Word' of God to large masses of people who, under this influence, experience what Protestants call conversion, salvation, regeneration, or spiritual rebirth."[2]

With the historical foundations of this revival now set in place, we can study its contemporary expression. What stands out with remarkable clarity is that on the one hand, the scholars within evangelicalism continued to pursue the holders-pressers debate to the point where by the decade's end, they had achieved not a single voice but instead, a bitter, no-compromise stalemate among themselves. Yet at the same time, a genuine revival broke out on the popular level (discussed later in Part Three), enveloping perhaps millions of seekers. Granted that no two major revivals in America have been reasonably identical, this twin personality of the movement stands as a unique and unprecedented phenomenon, leaving very serious doubts (discussed in Ch. XV) as to whether evangelical revivalism could survive into the future in any but the most rudimentary form.

To substantiate that prediction, we need persuasive evidence. That which is provided in Part Two assumes that the impetus for change and adjustment (the ripple effect) emerges first from the scholars and then spreads out to reach the masses. Hence, the evidence in Part II centers on the battles and divisions among the more reflective leaders, and how their battles turned not into a source of inspiration for the populace at large where a large harvest of souls was occurring but rather into a harvest of stalemate.

EVANGELICALS AND INERRANCY

No one gave a Grand Opening Party. No leader started to talk about bringing America back to Christ. No single spokesman came forward as the recognized great leader in the tradition of a George Whitefield, Dwight L. Moody, or the younger Billy Graham. Yet somewhere in the 1970s a fresh revival came on the scene soon to overshadow the other parts of the nation's religious life. Made up of a kaleidoscope of celebrities, programs, organizations and controversies, it was decidedly evangelical in character. In recognition of that fact, Newsweek magazine labelled 1976 "The Year of the Evangelical." And, as the evidence would suggest, that kind of instant historical labelling proved to be accurate.

On the popular level the statistical evidence included items such as the large increase in enrollment at evangelical colleges, seminaries and Bible schools, and "Christian day schools"; the boom in sales of books, cassette tapes and records with evangelical themes; the instant success of new evangelical television programs; and escalating enrollment in a variety of parachurch programs including Basic Youth Conflicts, Total Woman Seminars, Campus Crusade for Christ, Inter-Varsity Christian Fellowship and Marriage Encounter. Freely shared stories of personal conversion became assets rather than liabilities to public officials. Small, intentional communities of evangelical Christians appeared in significant numbers for the first time. Voluntary programs to work with the oppressed and exploited, and outcasts of society attracted considerable, if uncountable, evangelical participants.

The causes for such a revival were to be found in the events of the last 20 years, converging now in the mid-1970s as historian Donald Tinder suggested, into a unique configuration. First, evangelicals had by then built up the time, energy, and money to carry out such programs, ingredients they had not known to such a degree in their past. Secondly, many seekers found the more liberal Protestant teachings and programs no longer met their needs, hence they found new homes. Finally, the evangelicals had been able to modify their older, holy roller negative public image by utilizing new styles and approaches to traditional evangelism.

Tinder summarizes: "Evangelicalism, therefore, has blossomed not because it is new but because it was ignored for so long by outsiders. It flourishes because the institutions that give it visibility have only lately reached maturity. It appears to prosper more than it otherwise would because other expressions of Protestantism have lost some of the preeminence that they enjoyed for two or three generations. And it flourishes because, though conserving the doctrines at the heart of Christianity, it is innovative in a variety of other ways."[3]

So a revival by 1976 was underway. Yet, contrary to earlier ones, this found little leadership or instruction from the traditional source of scholars. They instead moved at an increasingly rapid pace into a position of division, acrimony and mistrust. A struggle of such magnitude, obviously, could emerge into public view only

after it had gone through considerable prior skirmishing over what
issues were in dispute. Its single most influential source emerged
from the appearance in the 1950s of a revitalized scholarly understanding of the older tradition, now named "neo-evangelicalism."[4]

Never an organized body, this movement centered on the new
research of scholars to make the evangelical voice respected and
influential in the larger world of religious scholarship. Weary of
the frequent and often unjust attacks on evangelicalism as being
in the 50s the same as the older, pugnacious and anti-intellectual
fundamentalism of the 1920s and 1930s, its leaders knew their tradition needed a responsible, convincing expression of its argument.
To that end, many of the new wave of leaders had pursued their
graduate studies in the more prestigious, nationally recognized seminaries and divinity schools. There, by contrast to earlier scholars
coming out of fundamentalist schools, the new evangelicals were required to work their way through a much different series of questions, assumptions and methodologies in religious studies, including
approaches to the study and interpretation of scripture which lay
far outside the earlier areas of concern.

Perhaps the most specific field challenging these scholars was
the widely accepted use of the historical-critical method of Biblical
texts. This method, widely accepted already by more centerist and
liberal seminaries had heretofore been avoided by evangelicals. Now
this new generation faced it directly. The field of hermeneutics,
or the principles one should use to interpret scripture, posed the
most challenging questions to the new generation. By using the historical-critical method they were forced to rethink what they had
been taught about the uniqueness and accuracy of the scriptures
as the directly inspired Word of God. Specifically, they reconsidered
such long-time interpretative problems as the factuality of the
Genesis creation narratives, the historicity of Jonah, the author-
ship of Isaiah and Hebrew (among others), the puzzle of how Moses
could write his own obituary, the canonical purposes of including
the Song of Solomon and Ecclesiastes, the reasons for the sharp

differences between the Gospel of John and the synoptic gospels, and the meaning of the Book of Revelation.

In short, they had to ask to what extent could human scholarship in archeology, linguistics, history and related fields be utilized to deepen and refine their understanding of a given text or resolve apparent factual errors or thematic contradictions. Was it possible the older fundamentalist interpretations were culturally conditioned interpretations, thus no more defensible than later, more liberal ones? Could the Bible, as the old saying had it, be read "for faith from faith"? Why was it not simply a magnificent collection of early Jewish history, prose, poetry, drama and wisdom literature akin to similar writings of other major would religious systems?

These kinds of questions met the evangelical scholars in the 1950s, and they came to realize many of the older answers would have to be reconsidered. What they nor anyone else could know then, was that the awakening of the 60s lay just ahead, that transformation would in its concern for the momentous public issues of the day demand from evangelicals fresh, authoritative biblical answers. In other words, new evangelicals familiar with the historical-critical method would find the need to interpret scriptural teaching on issues which their predecessors had not had to consider; racism, sexism, energy depletion, war and the like. Out of this milieu would emerge both the holders fast, who though understanding the new scholarship continued to follow more familiar hermeneutical pursuits, and the pressers on, equally at home in the new criticism but seeing in it the means to establish solid scriptural foundations for their social concerns.

The pressures from the holders fast to keep traditional answers at the center would clash with the pressure from those seeking to take such learning out of the ivory tower and the local parish and apply it to the escalating crises of the world. The question they asked, but could not solve collectively, was: "How do evangelicals translate their understanding of Biblical authority from theory into practice?"[5]   Those who insisted that no new critical

scholarship or pressure for social change was needed used as their
authority the school of thought known as the "verbally, fully inspired, inerrant, infallible Bible." Those ready to reconsider older
answers in light of the public crises rejected that position, producing instead several alternatives to the "inerrancy question."
Not ever holder fast espoused total inerrancy; nor did every press-
er on uphold one of its alternatives. But, on balance, it is fair
to suggest that inerrancy and holding fast fit together compatibly,
as did some alternative with pressing on.

But those were positions not yet visible when in 1956 the energy of the new evangelicalism led to the publication of the first
issue of Christianity Today. It stated its position: "The Bible is
the authoritative disclosure of God's word and purpose and thus
is the rule of faith and life." At the same time a new group just
founded, the Evangelical Theological Society (an umbrella organization for many in the new movement) made its affirmation: "The
Bible alone, and the Bible in its entirety is the Word of God written, and therefore inerrant in the autographs." [6] The key word
there is "inerrant" meaning that all biblical utterances are error-
less, not just those expressing the central teachings of salvation
and morals. The statements also rested on the assumption that the
Protestant Bible of 66 books was the final word from God. He had
revealed everything mankind needed to know and believe about His
redemptive work. No additional absolute truth from any Pope, council, or theologian would be forthcoming.

This position raised several questions, most of which still
keep evangelicals at their debating posts. What of the obvious dis-
crepancies, mistranslations, theological tensions between authors,
and factual errors in the Bible? [7] How literally could the Bible be
accepted when it talks about scientific matters or issues not related to God's saving work in Christ through the Holy Spirit? Would
it not be true that the Bible could be understood in part as a human book, embracing poetry, drama, wisdom literature, inspirational writing and prophecy?

Before the early 1970s, most evangelical spokesman publically answered these and similar questions with a cohesive, if not totally uniform, set of answers. The first was "plenary" inspiration; each of the 66 books was equally inspired by God; none had less validation as the words of God than any others. This rested on the assumption that God cannot err, otherwise He would not be God; God's revelation to mankind in the Bible means therefore that the Bible cannot err. The apparent factual errors were not present in the autographa, the first edition. Whatever errors exist today (and they are few indeed, as scholars have refined a more pure text from the original languages) are due to mistranslations and mistakes made by copyists from earlier translations. True, the first editions no longer exist so that today's editions cannot be collated with the originals. But the disappearance of the autographa is God's will, and must be accepted. Further, no one has seen "errant" first editions, just as no one has seen "inerrant" ones.

Another question involved was that because of mankind's sinful nature and self-centeredness, will not one's reason be clouded and distort the ability to determine inerrant truth? Carl F.H. Henry replied that the self-revealing God was rational and revealed Himself "rationally, that is, in intelligible propositions." Man has sufficient reason to trust his understanding of God once inerrancy of the Bible is accepted. This inerrancy is the starting point from which to penetrate the mysteries of God. In other words, no factual or literal error exists in the words of the Bible "in all that it affirms."[8] Third is the teaching of infallibility. Briefly, this means that God superintended the actual writing of each word of scripture; hence no higher authority for ultimate truth than the Bible exists. The Bible, in its original form, was inerrant and infallible.

Such a position was claimed by evangelicals to be the norm throughout the centuries until under the pressures from humanistic scholarship, the position was redefined and developed by scholars at Princeton Theological Seminary in the 19th Century, the "Princeton Theology." There verbal, plenary inspiration, along with inerrancy and infallibility were spelled out in a manner which most

new evangelical scholars accepted until the 1970s. However, once
the holders-pressers contest erupted, two evangelical scholars in
1979 produced a massive investigation of that claim, concluding
that the Princeton teachings were not the norm for hermeneutical
understanding and biblical authority.[9] But that moves us too far
ahead of the historical record.

The final doctrine dividing evangelicals would come to be that
of "verbal inspiration", spelled out first at Princeton. This position
held that God revealed Himself not only in the world of nature, not
only in the person of Christ but in the verbal (or written) words
of the 66 books. God did not dictate these words as to a steno-
grapher. But He inspired each author as the words were written
down. Each word in the original autographa was precisely the word
God intended. For proof the Princeton, and later evangelical scholars cited especially II Tim. 3:16 (as well as John 10:34-5): "All
scripture is given by inspiration of God, and is profitable for doctrine, for reproof, for correction, for instruction in righteousness."

The key word is "inspiration"; in Greek it is theopeneustos,
literally "God breathed out." In Princeton doctrine God did breath
out the words, revelation was verbal, not only general (as in nature or the Incarnation). God inspired every word (plenary inspiration) in such a manner that every word of every book fit together
in the manner He intended.

Verbal inspiration raised the question of how this happened;
what was the process? Scholars following the Princeton teachings
up until this day agree that no one has yet, or probably will be
able to explain just how the breathing out took place. Somehow God
worked in the life of each author, turning that person into an inspired writer, into a state of understanding the author did not
have in other moments of his life. Prof. Gordon Clark spelled this
out; verbal and plenary inspiration, inerrancy and infallibility
are beliefs "which the Holy Ghost Himself produces on our minds."
An unbeliever could not understand that process since the unbeliever lacked the power of the Holy Spirit to guide him into greater
insight. "So, too," Clark wrote, "when anyone accepts the Bible as

the Word of God he is not conscious of any break in the psycholog-
ical process." It is better (so it seems to me) to say simply that
God produced the belief in the mind."[10]

Such was the general consensus (with important exceptions)
until the early 1970s. Then, (as we have glimpsed already in this
book) the long-growing tensions between holders and pressers ex-
ploded. The immediate, specific issue was nothing less than one
of the decade's most bitterly disputed questions; the demands by
women and supporting men for full equality at work, at home, in
the schools and in the churches. For several years a handful of
evangelical scholars had been reexamining scripture to discover
whether the older tradition of Divine Order (esp. Eph. 5:22-6:9)
was truly biblical teaching.[11] Two landmark books by pressers
on, Letha Scanzoni and Nancy Hardesty, All We're Meant To Be
and Paul K. Jewett, Man as Male and Female challenged the methods and conclusions of the holders fast who who used the Bible as
their authority to relegate women to a secondary position. These
scholars insisted that the careful use of all accepted scholarly
tools, including the historical-critical method, for explaining what
the scriptures taught led to the conclusion that the submission-
inferiority position of women was unbiblical. Further, Jewett suggested that the cultural norms existing in the times of Paul (author
of Ephesians) shaped that missionary's teaching on women more
than did plenary inspiration. "In a word, Paul was wrong!"[12] That
conclusion was a direct refutation of evangelicalist teaching on inerrancy, and it had been made by a professor at one of the cita-
dels of evangelical scholarship, Fuller Theological Seminary.

Noting these and other signs of deviation from traditional
teachings and exegetical interpretations, the holders fast in 1976
made their response; the attack was led by Harold Lindsell, editor-
in-chief of Christianity Today. Drawing on research collected for
several years on the only slightly submerged inerrancy question,
Lindsell now decided to go public. In a book, The Battle for the
Bible, he took the leadership for those who would allow no scrip-
ural "errors" of any kind to be admitted. Linsell insisted "on the

inerrancy of the autographs of Scripture in every detail of chron-
ology, geography, astronomy, measurement and the like, even when
such details are incidental to the central intent of the passage."[13]
By "error" he meant any "mistatement or something that is contrary
to fact." This led him, as Robert K. Johnston, the most careful historian to date of the inerrancy battle, to conclude that Lindsell was
thus led to state, for example, that the cock crowed six times to
harmonize conflicting Gospel accounts of that event in Jesus' life;
that to harmonize the differences in the number of people who died
as stated in Numbers 25: (24,000) and Paul's different number
(23,000) in I Cor. 8:10 the answer must be "about 23,500."[14]

Beyond that, Lindsell traced what he understood to be the
decline of inerrancy in several evangelical seminaries and denominations. His major premise was that once total inerrancy is not
maintained (by weeding out deviant faculty, or insisting that they
sign inerrancy-loyalty oaths) then nothing will be left on which
to hold. The evangelicals will slip directly into the camp of the
liberals and ecumenicals whose scholarship differs so radically from
theirs. Once an evangelical said Paul was "wrong", then the end
times for that scholar and his institution had come unless remedial
actions are taken.

Strong as those indictments were, Lindsell went further by
stating in print what most holders fast had not expressed in public
before. Only those who affirmed the teachings of inerrancy as defined in his book deserved to wear the badge of "evangelical".
From so high and respected an authority, and with its endorsement
by at least two towering evangelical leaders, Harold John Ockenga
and Billy Graham, Lindsell's judgment fell like a thunderbolt over
the entire evangelical community. Denying the identity of being an
evangelical to the non-inerrancy scholars was tantamount to im-
pugning their personal faith; a stronger judgment could hardly be
made. Lindsell acknowledged that "belief in an infallible Scripture
is not necessary for salvation."[15] But he left no doubt that evangelicals must either commit themselves to total inerrancy, rejecting
the Jewetts and others, or lose their place within the ranks. It was
an either/or, love it or leave it ultimatum.   Holders fast and

pressers on were forced to come out of the closet and choose sides to a degree never before apparent in revivalist history.

Obviously, no reliable method exists to determine how many evangelicals supported and how many had moved into one of the other schools of thought which Lindsell found inadequate (Johnston lists these as "Irenic Inerrants", "Complete Infallibilitists" and "Partial Infallibilitists").[16] Lindsell's school, known as "Detailed Inerrantists", undoubtedly collected strong and widespread support when it was endorsed by Francis A. Schaeffer, founder and director of a Christian study community in Switzerland named L'abri (French for shelter) and a highly influential evangelical author and critic of culture. Schaeffer had made known in 1974 his loyalty to total inerrancy in a speech to the International Congress on World Evangelism in Lausanne. Shortly after that he toured the evangelical lecture circuit in America, basing his apologetic for evangelical teachings not only on traditional positions such as the Princeton theology but on his interpretations of Western art, music, and literature. A publisher found that public interest in Schaeffer was so great that the latter's lectures along with illustrative materials were placed on cassette tapes for wide distribution, followed later by a filmstrip series, "How Should We Then Live." While often criticized sharply by fellow evangelical scholars, Schaeffer's appearances now received wide public support. Audiences apparently found in him what they decided was a pure intellectual Christian who could outmatch the subtle arguments of those outside the inerrancy camp. The more sophisticated arguments of a Lindsell or other total inerrantists now reached the general public in a form which it understood and endorsed.[17]

The Lindsell position quickly attracted a powerful backlash of criticism from a wide variety of evangelicals. For instance, Donald Dayton found Lindsell's historical analysis to be "simplistic and dichotomous," largely ignoring earlier contrary evidence. To Dayton, Lindsell's attempt to link his argument in an unbroken link back to Princeton, the Westminster Confession, Calvin and Paul simply did not hold up; the evidence was missing. More important,

Dayton stated, evangelical faith was not based so heavily, as Lindsell had insisted, on using the Bible to draw up a system of propositional doctrines which followed in logical progression. Dayton argued that the message of the New Testament must be "extracted from first century 'cultural clothing'" to be intelligible to readers in the 1970s.[18]

Other major voices contributed rebuttals to Lindsell. Carl Henry wrote that the editor had failed to convince the audience that he (Lindsell) had uniting motives in mind as the book had claimed; the work was simply too much an unnecessary polemic. Henry pointed out that Lindsell's claim that the scriptures taught their own inerrancy offered no supporting texts for substantiation. Indeed, Henry said, "scriptural documentation is conspicuously absent." He also rejected Lindsell's demands to expunge the historical-critical method from evangelical seminary curricula. Above all, Henry rejected Lindsell's thunderbolt of removing the evangelical badge from the non-inerrancy people. Henry as he wrote in 1976 saw that this would create an unnecessary division among evangelicals, a split that could do only harm. As it turned out, Henry's prediction was to come true.[19]

Dayton and Henry were soon joined by other critics, Bernard Ramm, James Daane and others. All around, the division was extremely painful not only because of personal friendships but also because evangelicals had for decades claimed that their explanation of biblical authority was one of their most priceless treasures within Protestantism. Now it had been shattered and the issues would have to be aired openly without regard for individual feelings.

Lindsell's group now made its reply to its critics. Some 30 spokemen met in Chicago in October of 1977 to create "The International Council on Biblical Inerrancy." They intended to educate the evangelical community as to the importance of the doctrine, to expose their critics' weak arguments and to effect "institutional changes within seminaries, denominations, mission agencies, and other Christian organizations". Attendance was by invitation, led by Pastor James M. Boice of the Tenth Presbyterian Church of Philadelphia. Among the best known in attendance were Schaeffer, Ockenga, Bill Bright and Robert Preus of The Lutheran Church-- Missouri Synod where a kind of inerrancy war was being waged. Critics now criticized these critics, claiming the evangelical world needed no internal internecine battles while so much other work needed to be done. Fuller Seminary responded by authorizing the publication of a non-inerrancy position study Biblical Authority edited by Jack Rogers.[20]

But the door was open, the scholars were at battle and no one seemed able to work out a compromise until Prof. Robert K. Johnston in 1979 brought out his irenic book, Evangelicals at an Impasse: Biblical Authority in Practice. He suggested a set of hermeneutical guidelines as a way of mediating the differences. Lindsell promptly made a rebuttal in The Bible in the Balance in which he conceded nothing to his critics.[21]

Interestingly, the most reflective and constructive peacemaking efforts came from now the third editor of Christianity Today, Dr. Kenneth S. Kantzer, formerly dean at Trinity, Deerfield. (Henry and Lindsell had been the first and second editors.) Himself an expert biblical scholar, Kantzer called on evangelicals to continue their research, letting their faith shine as a light rather than hiding it when under criticism. Picking up on the issue of the "badge" of evangelical identity, he asked that inerrancy, to him "the most sensitive of all issues to be dealt with in the years immediately ahead," not be made a "test for Christian fellowship." The word "evangelical" had different meanings to different people, Kantzer continued, and thus should not be used too restrictively.

Kantzer made a plea that inerrancy should not be neglected as a major ingredient in evangelical belief; those institutions which required its profession for holding office or for ordination should continue to do so. Yet, the inerrancy question must be seen as being informed by the lordship of Christ and His authority; so long as Christ is Lord its place among believers will not weaken their witness. In brief, each generation must set forth its understanding

of all the issues and all of the ingredients of faith in terms meaningful to it; i.e., inerrancy is not true nor is it dated simply because the Princeton scholars once said it was true.

Kantzer asked for a cessation of personal criticism made outside of love for one another. The participants would benefit from
remembering Lindsell did not invent the controversy; it stretched
as far back as Calvin. The editor made several specific suggestions
for reconciliation, centering mostly on the need for greater clarity
of definition, of the recognition that ambiguity would always be
involved in such controversies, and of accepting the need to utilize
the best new biblical scholarship.[22]

Kantzer's proposals came at a time when the battle was moving out from academia and into the denominations, the ripple effect. Already, the International Conference on Biblical Authority
had published a summary of its second meeting (this again in
Chicago in October, 1978) -- a statement making no concessions to
any outside the Lindsell camp. The full Conference report appeared
in 1980, Inerrancy: The Extent of Biblical Authority, edited by
Norman Geisler. In 1980 the Southern Baptist Convention found itself in a fierce battle over the issue with contests for leadership
positions centering on loyalty to inerrancy. The controversy had
penetrated rank and file membership, leaving the SBC factionalized
and confused over the dangers of yielding too much or else defin-
ing "evangelical" too narrowly.[23] Entering 1980 Henry, the recognized, unofficial senior spokesmen for the entire tradition, wrote
more in sadness than anger that the controversy "will not go away.
It seems, rather to be building toward a day of institutional up-
heaval." Just as it had finally gained widespread public interest
and acceptance, Henry saw the advance retreating over an issue
that need not have produced such a result.[24]

Thus, this battle had no victors, only survivors. Such seems
inevitable to outside observers. When the strength and loyalty of
a cherished traditional position--evangelicism--collided with the
power and militancy of the 60s awakening and sophisticated schol-
arship--the historical-critical method--the splattering of bodies was

inevitable. Perhaps, if nothing else, the controversy illustrates how difficult, if not impossible, it is for humans to contain the essence of religious faith in human language. Yet the battle continues, even today.

CHAPTER VI

MALE AND FEMALE: THE EVANGELICAL STALEMATE

Through the smoke and din of the larger battle over the Bible, holders and pressers engaged in a wide-ranging series of contests over specific issues. These had developed out of the awakening of the 60s, demanding far reaching social change and the determination of some evangelicals to hold fast. Nowhere was the contest more vividly displayed than over the questions of human sexuality. Ch. VI discusses the general contest and ch. VII focuses on specific issues.

The initiative for the conflict was seized by the pressers on. They aimed at nothing less than overturning the traditional evangelical teachings and practice of women, specifically as wife, to accept her role as helpmate, submissive and unequal to the husband. Although evangelicals had been struggling over this issue for at least a century,[1] the holders fast position had dominated up until the 1960s. Then, with the public becoming increasingly accepting of open discussion of sexual matters, the pressers on made their move. Their decision to attack was influenced strongly by two broad sources. The mass media especially television, helped create the impression that a rapidly growing number of people's lives were highly sexual and glamorous, filled with a voracious appetite for forbidden fruit. What had been once considered stable in sexual behavior now appeared dated; what had once been regarded as daring was portrayed as the norm for the new age.[2]

A second source emerged from the impact in the mid–1970s of the woman's movement. Now, increasing numbers of feminists demanded more day care centers to allow mothers the opportunity to hold a job or more leisure time; more consciousness raising groups among women were formed; women also formed their own caucuses within political parties or professional associations. The sides were drawn, the battle underway.

Evangelicals, loyal to their tradition, chose to draw their heaviest artillery from the Bible. Pressers and holders recognized that unless their respective positions could be supported by scripture they could not carry the contest. The pressers, as Robert Johnston shows clearly, concentrated on "the broader affirmations of the gospel which stress oneness in Christ." Holders selected specific texts, especially from the Old Testament and the epistles, which established concrete rules. In that sense the battle was closely allied to the battle over the Bible; each side chose its set of hermeneutical principles, neither was willing to compromise.[3] The questions they raised focused on the interpretation of the Genesis accounts of creation; the teachings and actions of Christ towards women; the question of whether Paul's bias against women was divinely inspired (hence, inerrant and infallible) or a part of his rabbinical education; the meaning of the lives of the women of the Bible; and the extent to which evangelicals in today's world should be bound by the teachings of the early church fathers.[4]

Our examination of the contest will center on the conflicting answers to these questions offered by both sides, drawing in case study fashion on the most influential and responsible positions of each. For the pressers this would include such names as Nancy Hardesty, Letha Scanzoni, Virginia Mollenkott, Lucille Sider Dayton, and Paul K. Jewett. Holders would include George W. Knight III, Elisabeth Elliot, Thomas Howard, and Pat Brooks.

The foundational question is whether the physical differences between females and males as examplified in the different role each sex plays in reproduction and the rearing of children does create

a fixed order in nature which is God's will and which scripturally
fixes the roles and power granted by God to each sex. The holders
explain that since God rules this earth, He has allowed, as the record of history shows, men to be the rulers, leaders and protectors.
This proves that society has survived because it has respected this
  created order, with males in the dominant positions of power. Both
males and females have had enough time by now to give both sexes
the opportunity to prove what the created order of hierarchy between the sexes should be.

     Specifically, Howard finds in scripture, "a pattern of things
that is fixed by divine wisdom" and in the "hierarchical order,
rightly understood and enacted, freedom (or wholeness or felicity)
for each participant would be found in a set of relationships
reaching up and down." Elliot finds this order prescribed in the
first three chapters of Genesis. Females have their distinctive nature; God has called them to fulfill that nature. "It is our destiny, planned, ordained, fulfilled by an all-wise, all-powerful, all-
loving Lord." God the Creator made man in His own image, and saw
that something was missing. He decided man should not live alone.
God then created a helper, "specifically designed and prepared to
fill that role. It was a woman God gave man, a woman 'meet', fit,
suitable, entirely appropriate for him, made of his very bones and
flesh. This was the original idea. This is what woman was for."[5]
These conclusions are based on the holders' hermeneutical preference for accepting specific biblical texts rather than broad principles. The Bible said it, that should settle it.

     Pressers did not accept those answers. They started by ask-
ing different questions and using different hermeneutical principles.
Nancy Hardesty and Letha Scanzoni stated that everyone concerned
must constantly ask: What is the author really trying to say? What
is the historical context? Under what circumstances was the passage written? What do we know from history, archeology and other
fields that could shed light on the culture of the people to whom
a particular portion of scripture was addressed or from which it

sprang? How can this additional information help us better understand the meaning of the passage being examined? What is its ap-
plication for society and each individual? [6]

Starting with those questions, the pressers on reach different
conclusions. From Genesis (especially as developed by Jewett), they
find that if the woman were to have a secondary position, that
would deny her any "direct responsibility and relationship to God;"
it is simply wrong to hold that everything spiritual for the wife
is mediated through the husband. The traditional explanation of
the order of creation denies the fact that people see each other
as equals who do interact as responsible adults without preoccupa-
tion with some automatically assigned set or code of rules. The
Godhead cannot be and is not sexually differentiated; God is above
being a male or female. One finds no scriptural evidence for the
old claim that male is good, female as temptress is evil. The Bible
rather shows that both sexes depend upon one another and are un-
fulfilled until the humanity of both is accepted.   Nowhere does the
Bible teach that physical sexual differences must dictate social
roles. [7]

Thus holders and pressers divide over the first, most foundational source of God's revelation, the Genesis accounts. Both recognize that in Christ, a new creation has been bestowed, making the
older order obsolete. Thus they turn to the New Testament for their
evidence. They ask: What did Jesus teach about women? Elliot argues that we do know God chose to reveal a part of Himself as
male, in Jesus, and that Jesus chose only male disciples. Further,
Elliot writes, the whole ministry of Christ was one of sacrifice. To
a woman the acceptance of the husband as head is not a sacrifice,
but one of freedom from false and misleading scriptural teaching.
Couples are not really to be equal, "equality is not really a Christian ideal." The highest good for any servant of God is to glorify
Him and to submit to one's master just as Christ did. God is the
author of this authority, as seen in the Incarnation, and Jesus'
words. "All authority is given to me." Freedom is bestowed when

the believer takes up her or his cross and submits to that authority.[8]

In the same school, Pat Brooks argues that no earthly relationship, even marriage, can alter the freedom and excellence a
person (i.e., here, a woman) can know by faith in Christ. "Anyone can excel here, because the Lord Jesus is perfect." Yielding
to His will brings great joy because women are after all "daughters
of the King." Thus born again, radiant life transcends the mun-
dane quibbles over human struggles and power plays. The life triumphant to be consummated in eternal life is the victory for all
people.[9]

In response, Hardesty insisted that Jesus was indeed a feminist, seeing women as fully equal. It is true, she conceded, that
He did not quarrel in words with the authorities at that time who
kept women in roles of submission. But the clue to understanding
came from studying what Jesus did. Contrary to rabbinical practices, He talked about everyday experience in the lives of the women
as well as of men. He allowed women to travel with Him; and He
talked to women in all classes and stations of life. In John 12 He
failed to rebuke Martha for serving a roomful of men, something
a traditional woman would have left for a man servant to do; nor
did Jesus withdraw when Mary used her hair to dry His feet. Jesus
appeared first after the resurrection to women; they were the first
to know the good news. [10]

Mollenkott finds biblical feminism supported in the doctrine
of the new creation in Christ. Those in Christ (II Cor. 5:17) are
new creatures; those baptized in Christ (Gal. 3:27) have put on
Christ; those called to liberty (Gal. 5:13) are by love to serve one
another. Women at Pentecost obviously fulfilled the prophecy of Joel
(Joel 2:28-30) by prophesying. In disagreeing with the Pharisees
over the traditional teaching on divorce (Matt. 19:3-9), Jesus showed
"that sacred scripture concerning man's behavior towards woman
does not always reflect God's highest intentions for the human
race." [11] That conclusion was indeed extremely far removed from traditional loyalty to the Bible.

The other major source of tension in the battle has been differing interpretations of the teachings of Paul regarding the role of women. For centuries the most widely accepted evangelical understanding of passages such as Eph. 5:22 and 6:1 and I Cor. 11 had been fully literal; wives submitting themselves to their husbands as to the Lord; husbands, to love their wives, but without reference to submitting themselves to their wives. Paul admonished women to cover their heads since they are "the image and glory of God." Finally (among the many passages that could be cited) wom-were not allowed to speak in church but to be in submission.

From this Elliot concludes, in explaining Gal 3:28 where Paul wrote about there being "neither male nor female" that this passage must be seen in conjunction with other Pauline statements where he, as in I Timothy accepts the order of creation, "Let a woman learn silence with all submissiveness. I permit no woman to teach or to have authority over man; she is to keep silent. For Adam was formed first, then Eve." Hence the Galatians passage "refers to what happens to a Christian through baptism. He becomes, whether male or female, slave or free, Jew or Greek, a son." [12]

That interpretation satisfied the holders regarding final authority. But pressers on insisted that Paul was saying something rather different. Using their hermeneutical guidelines, they found that Paul, in talking about covering the head, was following the carefully prescribed Jewish practices. Regarding women not preaching, Paul again was following the Talmud. The newly converted Jews had not yet been able at that time to absorb fully the idea of equality into their values. Regarding I Timothy about women learning in silence, the pressers on state that Paul was there concerned with the cultural status quo, addressing himself to a specific immediate and local situation. Paul was not laying down for all time a principle about women's roles in the churches. Apparently, pressers point out, in that congregation some untrained women were trying to teach heresy, which added confusion to the group. [13]

Further feminist-pressers arguments pointed out that existing translations such as the King James were biased against women; as seen in I Tim. 2:11 about "in silence" which should be translated as "quietly". They suggested that not even in patriarchal Israel was the male always dominant, a clear "depatriarchalizing tendency" was to be found in the Song of Solomon, Exodus 20:12 and Deut. 5:16. This was continued in the New Testament expressed forcefully in Gal. 3:28. Further, Paul explained the position of women (e.g., in Ephesians) in terms the readers could understand by comparing it to the slavery of the times. Pressers asserted such teachings were only to be analogous; God could not have endorsed slavery for all times. [14]

The holders responded with more scripture and more rebuttals from the historical record. They considered the woman's movement to be only a present-day cultural fad; otherwise, if it were so biblical, why had it not been expressed fully before the secular woman's movement came into the arena? Throughout all of scripture, males were the leaders; one could not ignore the full witness of scripture. Further, God chose to establish Christ as the head of the church, and hence a male must be the head of the home; in that manner His divine authority, dominion and supremacy were accurately explained.[15]

Beneath all these arguments, as Johnston shows, rested convictions, personal preferences and conflicting loyalties which could not be resolved. Throughout the war no one was saying that "the truth lies somewhere in the middle." Once committed to either the holders' or pressers' positions, leaders would have to remain loyal to the answers they reached by following their respective principles. Johnston himself tried during the heat of the battle to establish some "interpretative principles" for guiding the perplexed readers who could not understand the nuances and assumptions of the antagonists. Among these were a plea that each text be studied "within its full unit of meaning," not simply taking one verse here or there; some translations had a sexist bias and must be corrected; students must always keep the literary form of any text foremost as must its historical context; everyone concerned should understand the author's biblical methods, stated intentions and theology in light of parallel texts, thus eliminating the "multiple theological foci" of scripture and holding up instead its "overarching consistency."

Johnston also pleaded for relying on texts where the meaning is clear rather than those more obscure; he repeated the familiar evangelical dictum that the Bible must be read in faith for faith. Students should draw on all of the resources of the church, and finally they must remember that there will be no additional inerrant, infallible, inspired writings; hence interpretations today must accept the fact that changes in interpretation will be forthcoming, "progressive revelation", but that the Bible is still the final authority.[16]

For what it is worth, by 1980 the momentum for following progressive revelation came to reside clearly with the pressers on. They organized groups within congregations, in cities, in states and in denominations, and nationally to continue their battle. Examples would be the Evangelical Women's Caucus and the Daughters of Sarah, and a newsletter "Free Indeed." Articles favorable in their position appeared frequently in mainline church publications as well as in such evangelical journals as The Other Side, Sojourners, and The Wittenburg Door. By contrast, holders fast remained content to repeat their positions, but not to organize in any comparable systematic manner. There is no World Conference on Divine Order as exists for upholding inerrancy (see p. 56). By 1980 no fresh, new arguments were appearing from either camp; the major arenas for the battle had been drawn, the weaponry selected and the combatants hard at it. No satisfactory method exists by which to gauge how many evangelicals favored either position. So, by contrast to the inerrancy question which lends itself more accurately to numerical measurement, we can only conclude that those who support the pressers on have been heard, rebutted, but they go on. The battle has turned into a stalemate.

CHAPTER VII

THE HOLD AND PRESS IN THE PUBLIC ARENA

The collision of the 60's awakening and the evangelical revival of the next decade forced the spokespersons of the latter to reconsider not only their hermeneutics and teachings on sexuality, but every major social issue of the era. Only three of these can be considered here, chosen because each logically follows from the general subject of the last chapter. These are: The Equal Rights Amendment, legalized abortion, and the civil rights of homosexuals. To some Americans, including evangelicals, all three were interrelated; a vast conspiracy was at work destroying traditional norms. Obviously no such plot existed, but the perceived belief that a direct connection among them did exist helped to intensify the heat if not the light on these complex problems.

Evangelicals had long stood indicted by their critics and a few of their own for lacking a sustained interest in social questions. Much of that indictment could be and was documented by the leaders themselves for several years before the new revival. As early as 1947 Henry was writing about The Uneasy Conscience of Modern Fundamentalism followed by related evaluations from David O. Moberg, Bernard Ramm, E.J. Carnell, Lewis Smedes and others. On the surface the battle seemed clear enough; evangelicals must work to win souls for Christ, and not involve themselves in the compromising, secular realm of politics and social gospel do-goodism. Beneath that long-standing dispute, however, lay a wide variety of cultural, denominational, and ideological forces at work, keeping most evangelicals aloof from social involvement.[1]

Again, on the surface through the post World War II years, appearances suggested a virtually unanimous evangelical stance; politically conservative, economically devoted to the free market position, socially suspicious of most government (instead of voluntary) welfare programs. That consensus was first weakened as early as the first years of the 1970s leading, as we have seen, to the "Chicago Declaration" and "Evangelicals for McGovern" to name two early signs of change. Then in mid-decade the pressers on took the initiative on spelling out a series of alternative evangelical responses to those of the past; the consensus had been broken, and perhaps even shattered, as one of the three theses of this work posits. The pressers discovered that the united single voice from evangelical loyalty to the Bible no longer sufficed. Using both old and new hermeneutics they produced a series of social ethics answers which were a melange of conservative, moderate, reformist, and radical. By way of defense, they would insist that the biblical voice was equally multiple; they were only being true to the scriptural voice which defied the comfortable pigeonhole categories of the past.[2] The holders fast would not agree.

ERA

The proposed amendment reads: "1. Equality of rights under the law shall not be denied or abridged by the United States or by any State on account of sex. 2. The Congress shall have the power to enforce by appropriate legislation, the provisions of this article. 3. This amendment shall take effect two years after the date of ratification."

Proposed shortly after the women's movement made its presence known nationally, it attracted enormous attention in evangelical circles. The anti-ERA cause found its most effective leader not within evangelical ranks but with a Roman Catholic, Phyllis Schlafly. Well known in evangelical circles since her book supporting Senator Barry Goldwater for President (A Choice, Not an Echo) she took command of the forces to prevent its adoption. With six children,

being a full time student in law school, producing a monthly newsletter and speaking frequently across the country, she claimed (with
good reason) to speak up persuasively for the middle American.[3]

Evangelicals and others found her 1977 book The Power of the
Positive Woman to be the best single statement of their case.   She
appealed to evangelicals because she used scripture as her rockbed
source of authority. She pointed to Ephesians 5 and the Pauline
"wives, submit yourselves unto your husbands, as to the Lord" as
her primary prooftext. The Bible, she stated, taught the existence
of a "valid and enduring purpose behind this recognition of different roles for men and women," to her as relevant today as in
the time of Paul. She quoted scripture, "where there is no vision,
the people perish" as meaning that "America is the greatest country in the world and that it is her [America's] task to do her part
to keep it that way." Such a God-given task could never be
achieved were the nuclear family to yield to the dangers explicit
in the ERA. To her, women have been and are ready to answer the
call of Christ "to be His vehicle" to preach moral renewal and
Christian unity. For her model, Schlafly cited Saint Brigette, a 14th
century queen in Scandinavia. Obeying Christ, Brigette turned back
the corruption of adultry and abortion; so too in the 70s, the auth-
or insisted, today's Positive Woman must take up this task.[4]

Her message, her brilliant platform presence, and well organized local supporters brought out large crowds wherever she
spoke. The theme was usually anti-ERA but would move into anti-
abortion, anti-gay rights and similar crusades. Her case, stated
clearly in the February, 1972 issue of "The Phyllis Schlafly Report"
centered on these convictions. First, American women had more privileges, rights, rewards and opportunites than women anywhere else
in the world; ERA would take all that away. She reasoned that because the Judeo-Christian tradition requires that since women "must
bear the physical consequences of the sex act," men must be required to bear the other consequences, and pay with physical protection and financial support the costs of wife and children. Women
do not need jobs. From the 4th Commandment they understand that

their children are their best social security, the best guarantee of social benefits such as old age pension, unemployment insurance, workman's compensation and sick leave.

Second, because of the Christian Age of Chivalry, women in America benefit more from being placed on a pedestal more fully than is true in any other country. Other cultures such as the African and native American let the men "strut around wearing feathers and beads, hunting and fishing" while the real work is being done by women. Third, American free enterprise has produced great inventors whose work removed backbreaking toil from the lot of women; stoves, washers, refrigerators and the like --these are the liberators of women.

To Schlafly, ERA would destroy all the gains American women have. It would make women subject to combat duty; it would abolish a woman's right to child support and alimony in divorce; it would often take away custody of the children from the mother and give it to the father; it would deprive a woman of the right not to take a job, or to keep her child and be supported by her husband.

The pro-ERA arguments to her simply were not true. Women's "libbers" were, in her judgment, the radicals who hated men, celebrated lesbianism, ridiculed motherhood, supported abortion on demand, favored no restrictions on gays (including their right to marry), and the like. The sum total of changes under ERA would destroy American society.[5]

An equally determined, if less well organized pro-ERA movement emerged among evangelical and mainline church leaders. Among the best brief arguments made for the ERA, as our case study we will look at that made by the Rev. Constance F. Parvey and the Rev. Richard W. Rhyne in the November, 1975 issue of the journal, Lutheran Women.[6]

They start by stating the ERA harmonizes with the Declaration of Independence and the Gettysburg Address; hence it is hardly 'radical'. They insist the ERA would strengthen the nuclear family; a woman would have the right to choose whether or not to

work. ERA guaranteed that those who chose employment would have
the same guarantees and privileges as men, especially in wages
and positions of power. Parvey suggested that some anti-ERA sentiment came from businesses which did not want to pay equal wages
for equal work. From an explicitly Christian position she favored
ERA because in the believer's baptismal convent, the statement of
Paul in Gal. 3:28 about being neither male nor female meant "no
barriers of sexual, religious or economic discrimination have any
authority in the Body of Christ." She pointed to the freedom given
to Christians, as outlined in Romans 8. To live out this freedom,
she argued, people had to exercise it. "The Christian lifestyle demands unfailing vigilance over our freedoms right here and now."

Parvey argued that with freedom comes Christian responsibility, concern for one's neighbor's welfare (Rom. 15:2). That meant
ERA applied to everyone, "it touches the lives of other women;
failure to pass it hinders other women's exercise of their civil
rights." Without it, further stereotyping of differences between male
and female were being perpetuated; this meant less freedom and
a loss of everyone's sense of responsibility for everyone else. On
Pauline passages teaching submission, Parvey followed the pressers
on argument that Paul's mindset was shaped by the culture of that
day.

Rhyne reviewed the economic and social case for ERA, then
moved into a theological argument. As Christians, Americans are
"one in identity with God." That meant we look to the doctrine of
creation as the best biblical answer on this issue. There, glory
and manifold beauty were found, thus creation is good." Genesis
speaks of the total creation of God creating "male and female" in
equal partnership. God is a fellowship of persons (Father, Son,
Holy Spirit) just as "man" is intended to be a fellowship of persons
(male and female) not man in distinction to woman. It was not until after the fall that God gave Adam rule over Eve, and then only
as an act of Judgment for a specific act...." Further, four times
in the Old Testament God is referred to in non-male terms, but more
as a mother (Deut. 32:11, Is. 46:3, Is. 49:15, Psalms 131:2).

Christians are equal in their oneness, their unity in creation without rank or status.   God, not male, is superior; women and men are indispensible to each other through their ministry to each other and to the world. Today our laws do not yet, Rhyne argued, reflect that liberty. "Liberation is accepting your inheritance in Christ as a full partner."[7]

The arguments for both camps could be extended almost indefinitely. What was at stake here in the evangelical resurgence is of the greatest importance. The argument centers on the nature of authority. Would the pressers on help bring the world closer to collapsing; would holding fast retard justice; how can we separate out emotion from legal precedent, propaganda from fact? Evangelicals were discovering that fidelity to scripture was no guarantee that compelling arguments for a stated position would be axiomatic, which is one way to reach an impasse.

GAY RIGHTS

Much the same pattern of response by evangelicals to a second area of sexual identity, that of homsexuality, burst into public view in the mid-70s. For decades they had found a clear biblical mandate prohibiting any form of homosexual activity. Then, even while a substantial majority of evangelical laity continued to believe that, a small number of pressers on called for a reexamination of the traditional position. [8]

This issue emerged at that time in part because of the impact of the 60's awakening in which the theme of liberation from all past restrictions and freedom to be one's true self informed the activists' outlook. In the 70s many city councils passed resolutions or ordinances guaranteeing no discrimination against homosexuals regarding housing and employment. Specifically, this meant that practicing homosexuals could not be evicted from present or future neighborhoods on the grounds of their sexual behavior. It also meant that gays who were schoolteachers (to name one profession involved) could not be removed from their positions because of their sexual preference. Opponents to gays responded critically, stating that gays in a neighborhood would lower its property value and its reputation; parents of school children feared having gays as role models-teachers for their children.

Further complications arose within churches when seminary graduates, who were practicing homosexuals, requested to be ordained. Denominational bodies on the local, regional and national levels responded with in-depth studies. Few churches, however, actively supported gays; most called on members to show love, understanding and maintain traditional norms.

Among evangelicals, holders fast found in the leadership of Anita Bryant the kind of bold, no-nonsense, simple answer they quickly accepted as the norm. On the other side, as had happened with inerrancy and Divine Order issues, the pressers on divided into at least four camps, ranging from punitive up through qualified acceptance and on to full acceptance of "loving, committed homosexual relations."[9]

Bryant's arguments best reflected rank and file laity opinion. A lifelong evangelical, she found in the Bible the texts which when properly linked together furnished the authority to oppose all forms of homosexuality. Its practice was contrary to the clear teachings of right and wrong found in scripture. She cited both Old and New Testament adulterers, nor effeminate, nor abusers of themselves" being allowed into the Kingdom of God; and Lev. 20:13 about a man to lie with another man as he does with a woman committing an abomination; the punishment of God against Sodom and Gomorrah; and Romans 1:22-32 among other sources. Accepting the changing sexual behavior patterns in America of the time as a given fact, Bryant called on evangelicals and all citizens to draw the line here, to keep the family together against the powerful pressures for change. Were the nation to fail her, she feared Gcd would desert it and let it turn to rot as happened in Rome. To support her case she cited secular scholarship, a book by George F. Gilder, Sexual Suicide, which argued that homosexuality and lesbianism were ruining the family in America. Only a return to traditional sexual relationships could preserve Western society.[10]

Pressers on, however, could not accept Bryant's position; it was too superficial, too close to being punitive for their understanding of sexuality. Among the several scholars who searched for a more convincing approach, the writing of Professor Lewis Smedes in his Sex for Christians represented the qualified acceptance of homosexuality. Holding that gay behavior was something of a distortion of the biblical norm, Smedes pleaded with his readers to reject both total acceptance and total rejection. He argued that scripture does judge homosexual practice as godless and unnatural; it was rarely an expression of nurturing personal relationships, and its practice very often led to serious flaws in the total development of a gay's character. Smedes called on the readers to help homosexuals understand the abnormality of their situation but accepting the responsibility of creative use of their sexual energy. Gays could be helped by counseling and divine healing. If both fail, the homosexual should work out an "optimum homosexuality morality," accepting that as "preferable to a life of sexual chaos."[11]

Easily the most assertive and reflective position of another faction among the pressers on appeared in 1978 when Virginia Ramey Mollenkott and Letha Scanzoni brought out a book Is the Homosexual My Neighbor: Another Christian View.[12] Too complicated and detailed to be summarized briefly, the book used both biblical and behavioral science evidence to argue that homosexuality was not condemned in the scriptures to the degree its opponents claimed. They stated the scientific evidence finds the homosexual preference not to be one of deviance or pervasion, but a situation which medical science could treat successfully.

As evangelicals, the authors devoted considerable attention to the biblical record. They rejected the Bryant argument, using instead the historical-critical form of exegesis. For example, the sin of Sodom, Genesis 19, was violent gang rape, not the homosexuality of today; thus the injunctions from that scripture did not apply in the present. The prohibitions found in Leviticus 18 and 20 did refer to homosexual behavior. But, the authors state, these same passages also referred to other situations such as a ban on intercourse during a menstrual period -- thus the sting is taken out of the Leviticus passages.

Mollenkott and Scanzoni also analyzed the appropriate passages in Romans 1, I Corinthians, and I Timothy 1. On the first, they pointed out that Paul knew nothing about homosexual love, but was referring to lust and idolatry. In the other passages the authors' reference was to sexual abuses, temporary situations, not to lifelong homosexuality. They concluded with a statement showing how far from the holders fast position they had moved: "Since the Bible is silent about the homosexual condition, those who want to understand it must rely on the findings of modern behavioral science and on the testimony of those persons who are themselves homosexual."[13] The pressers on had made their break; they chose to utilize human scholarship on an issue which the holders fast found clearly enunciated in scripture alone.

Beyond the battle among the scholars, a tiny number of gays organized in the mid-70s themselves into "Evangelicals Concerned." This was a loosely connected network of some 12 chapters, producing a regular newsletter, sponsoring rap sessions and Bible studies. As they went public, no apparent organized form of discipline against them was taken by evangelical leaders, leading one careful observer to believe the movement would continue to grow slowly.[14]

As forthright as the pressers on position was, the holders fast by 1980 held the initiative in teachings concerning homosexuality. The overwhelming majority of evangelicals continued to believe that "no possible Scriptural support for even a qualified homosexuality" existed. In no way did the Bible explicitly support that sexual preference: "the Biblical mandate against homosexuality seems strong."[15] What no evangelical could answer, however, were questions such as supporting a sexual practice which to him was wrong, possibly creating more problems by showing tolerance

than standing fast. Or in civil rights, could a church-related
group such as the evangelicals demand the removal from a public
school of a teacher whose sexual lifestyle they rejected? Would
that breach the wall of separation of church and state were a
school board to allow special interest groups such as evangelicals
to dictate their hiring practices? The same general question applied also to discrimination in housing. Hence, an impasse; holding
fast was no longer as simple as it had been a few years back.

ABORTION

Without any doubt, the most controversial and least compro-
misable issue regarding human sexuality is that of abortion. No
issue in the 70s divided Americans more bitterly, none has had so
drastic an effect on American life. We have reached minus Zero
Population Growth. We soon learned the effects this had on public
school enrollment, and teaching career opportunities there for young
adults, as well as slowly but steadily creating an aging society,
which would have an enormous impact on the economy.

Many Americans insisted, after the Supreme Court decision of
1973 allowing abortion as a legal procedure under certain conditions concerning the length of life of the fetus, and properly li-
cenced health facilities, that the issue went far beyond school enrollment and the economy. It was a matter of life and death. At
the thousands of rallies, demonstrations and marches across every
section of the country, the placards read "Pro Life" or "Pro
Choice." Physical violence erupted at the marches, and extensive
damage was done to the property of abortion clinics. Families,
churches and communities have chosen sides; public funding of
abortions for the poor became a major political issue. The morality
of abortion splintered our society into increasingly bitter and un-
compromising armies.

Evangelicals with a few important exceptions (noted later)
came to stand strongly united on abortion. They rejected the Supreme Court decision, believing that once conception had taken

place, the fetus must be allowed to come to term and birth allowed. Anything short of that, to most of them, was simply murder. Some leaders acknowledge that in situations such as rape, incest or threatened damage to the health of the pregnant mother, then abortion might be a viable, if unpleasant alternative.

Yet the opinion makers also recognized that the situation was not totally either/or. They understood the complexity of questions such as the effect of unrestricted population growth on world resources and its ecology; or the lifelong tragedy which could occur from one moment of carelessness. Further, at what point does the fetus become a person? Does the fetus have rights? Is the Bible unmistakeably clear on these matters? Could not the attempt to prohibit abortion drive its practice underground, making it far less physically safe than is now the case?

No major evangelical spokesperson was willing to make a total condemnation of all abortions. An apparent majority of rank and file said the protection of life overshadowed all of the questions of resources, ecology and underground clinics. The evangelical community, by and large, supported the proposed constitutional amendment to outlaw the legalization of abortion in all but the most extreme situations. Interestingly, two highly placed evangelical leaders, Representative John Anderson of Illinois and Senator Mark Hatfield of Oregon, disagreed over such an amendment. Anderson argued that abortion does not belong in a political platform; it was too personal a human issue. Hatfield, however, argued that in the crusade to preserve human life, only a prohibitive constitutional amendment could stop the growing practice of abortion. He knew of no other legal means available.[16]

Other evangelicals pressed for allowing qualified acceptance. In Minnesota, for example, a leading abortion-rights activist and a deeply commited Christian, made her views known. She supported the Supreme Court decision because "knowing God is love" such knowledge, not flat prohibitions, must inform each situation as it appeared.[17] The evangelical writer and educator, Tim La Haye

noted, "The Bible is not clear as to when the fertilized egg becomes a person -- at the moment of conception, or when the embryo
develops into a fully formed human being at three to six months."
Obviously, if the fertilized egg is regarded only as a living cell,
that simplifies the task of approving some form of abortion. If that
egg is indeed a person the issue becomes more complicated. La
Haye approved therapeutic abortions for emergency cases, but rejected abortion for "all personal or selfish reasons."[18] Hardesty and
Scanzoni acknowledged the complexity of the question. They favored
the therapeutic solution, and endorsed the insights of a book sponsored by the Christian Medical Society: Salter O. Spitzer and
Carlyle L. Saylor, eds., Birth Control and the Christian.[19]

The summary here of the holders fast versus pressers on
battle need not be long. The single voice of evangelicalism within
American Protestantism could not be maintained following the
awakening of the 1960s. Once its impact was felt and the pressers
on accepted, in varying degrees, the historical-critical hermeneutic
they broke the traditional consensus. They did so, knowing well
what it would mean, yet believing that they were being as loyal
to scripture as were those within the family who held fast. Once
each side committed itself in print, it could not turn back. Too
much was at stake, not only in formal scholarship, but in actual
life situations. That cleavage was one fundamental ingredient which
made the revival of the late 1970s totally unique in American revival history. It thus reflected the complexity of the community of
faith which sought permanent, absolute truth and authority to be
applied to a world in constant motion and change.

PART THREE

AMERICAN REVIVAL: THE YEARS OF THE EVANGELICALS

1976-1980

CHAPTER VIII

1976: THE TAKEOFF YEAR

By its nature, religious faith is mankind's most inclusive, all-encompassing attempt to find meaning, order, direction and inspiration for everyday life. It touches, or can touch, every part of life: work, play, the arts, symbols, behavior, lifestyle, politics, business, education -- the list could be extended at length. It continues to attract the attention of psychologists, sociologists, historians, artists, scientists, archeologists, linguistic specialists -- again a very long list could be made.

Leaders of religious families, be they ministers or priests or scholars or opinion shapers seek to shape this faith into areas of commitment and expression which are understandable and meaningful to their followers. The lay people, in turn, have the opportunity to take all or parts or none of the leadership offered them. In the United States this kind of freedom has led to a vast variety of differing religious expressions, as complex and diverse as each individual involved. As indicated above, one such expression has been the revival, aimed at nothing less than a total transformation of the seeker in every aspect of his or her life. Revivals make extraordinary claims for transformation; a new life, a permanent meaning, an eternal timeless home are the results of the decision to be born again.

Timeless though their theology is, American revivals do take place within the immediate, historical setting of a given time, place and climate of opinion. Hence, no two revivals in our history have

been quite the same. They are in large part the product of their
culture. They reflect, for instance, the various levels of understanding and social class as well as the perennial individual
search for ultimate meaning.

What is the continuity and the variety of the revival of 1976–
1980? Its central thrust was that of every revival; to bring the
searcher to contrition, recognizing his helplessness before the all-
powerful God of judgment, yet open to receive the transforming
power of the Holy Spirit in conversion to enable him to put on a
new nature, freed from the fears of an eternal damnation. Yet this
revival was shaped and informed by its immediate context, hence
its dialectical nature.

Certainly this revival had its own personality, not the least
because as we have just seen, many evangelical opinion shapers
were locked in bitter internal battles. Theirs was the realm of the
college, the seminary, the library, from which evangelicalism had
long been nurtured. But in this revival the level of understanding
which settled at the popular level, exhibited many characteristics
of what Peter W. Williams defines as "popular religion"; first,
existing apart from or in tension with established religious groups
with regular patterns of organization and leadership; second, having its beliefs transmitted through channels other than the official
seminaries or oral traditions of established religious communities;
third, searching for signs of divine intervention or manifestations
in the realm of everyday experience.[1]

The 70's revival for several reasons qualifies for inclusion
as popular religion encompassing every part of life. First, the
broadest area of public concern was elective politics; the candidacy
of Jimmy Carter was the most explicitly born again in character
since William Jennings Bryan ran in the first part of the century.
Carter's presence made vivid to every American of whatever religious commitment the ongoing presence of evangelical involvement in
public life. Carter's candidacy (as will see in ch. XIII) was interpreted by some observers as part of the new revival.

Secondly, much of the 70's revival was spent in para-church programs, as will be discussed later, e.g., Basic Youth Conflicts, Total Woman Seminars, Christian day schools, the "electronic church" and other expressions. All of these reached out for as wide an audience as possible. Finally, the 70's resurgence was a revival because it placed enormous emphasis on the instant conversion, born again experience as being the only source of power able to transform daily lives. Popular evangelical faith was by the mid-1970s a major reflection of the nation's renewed understanding of itself.

But, it must be asked, why was the year 1976 the takeoff point? Why did events then break the logjam from which poured the revival? It would take more than the opinion of the editors of Time magazine to make that the beginning of "The Years of the Evangelicals." To be sure, no ribbons were cut, no kickoff mass rally for hundreds of thousands of believers was staged. Yet 1976 was the inaugural year in large part because of the candidacy and, eventually, the victory of Jimmy Carter as President.

His victory was more than a little incongrous; it made little sense according to the traditional political wisdom. Carter had held no national office, he had no experience in foreign policy and held few ties to the power brokers in Washington. He was enthusiastically a Southerner, the first major party finalist candidate in 64 years. And he lacked a large campaign treasure chest for the primaries.

Yet he won. Many observers wondered as did Albert Menendez, "Did Carter's religion help or hurt on balance? In the absence of scientific motivational analysis we cannot know for sure. I am inclined to think it helped a little more than it hurt."[2]

Carter's presence helped legitimize the motives of those evangelicals, mostly the pressers on, who had chosen in the 1970s to express their faith in the world of public decision formation and administration, thus breaking with the long-standing hands-off-of-politics attitudes of the holders fast. The intensity and the openness of Carter's public witnessing contributed to the other signs that the evangelicals were indeed finding acceptance and, for the first time, power in the larger American society.

So, 1976 stands as the takeoff year; the revival dominated the religious scene of the nation. As surprised as many observers were over its appearance, they need not have been. For at least six years important indications of an imminent revival were appearing. For instance, in 1970 the Gallup Poll showed that from 1957 and on, the percentage of persons believing that religion as a whole was increasing its influence on American life moved upward from 14 per cent to 75 per cent.[3] Beyond the statistics, the mainline churches were declining steadily in membership, attendance, financial support and social outreach.

The observers soon found reason. One located it in the loss of authority. The awakening of the 60s had convinced mainline members that they were growing in faith by experimental liturgies, informality in worship, being open-minded towards the latest anti-institutional church criticisms. In general these churches had reduced the distance of authority between minister and laity to zero. In keeping with the 60s theme of 'participatory democracy,' the ministers had no longer any claim to denomination authority or specialized educational insight into the faith. Thus, a standoff developed; no longer was there a locus of authority.[4]

In 1972 came one of the most far reaching and authoritative criticisms of mainline Protestantism and a clue to why evangelicals were growing in number. Dean Kelley, a high official of the National Council of Churches, explained with impressive statistical data, as he titled it, Why Conservative Churches are Growing.[5] As the zeal of the 60s for social activism faded away, the openmindedness towards all those dissenters of the earlier decade was apparently leading significant numbers of seekers to conclude that the mainline bodies really lacked any systematic body of convictions. In turn, Kelley showed, those bodies which demanded group solidarity, personal sacrifice and celebrated the free sharing of the good news of one's rebirth were gaining strength. Something was stirring just under the surface.

The initial answers concluded that those switching to evangelicalism were bored or discouraged with the mainline priorities of ending the Vietnam war, working with the oppressed, supporting the woman's movement, and tolerating the counterculture. Beyond that, one in-depth case study of a Lutheran Church in America congregation showed that the question most of its parishioners wanted answered in their parish was "how do we make people feel loved, cared for, wanted?"[6]

In a famous essay, "The ME Decade" critic Tom Wolfe offered a broad interpretation of what was stirring beneath the surface. The major, uniting social issues of the 60s were gone; the country's major governing institutions such as the schools, churches, government and business seemed unwilling or unable to hold the loyalty and manage the society. Hence, the one place, the one thing the seeker could do was turn inward, concentrate on his own development, restore his self identity and at least save himself, just in case this nation was actually sinking into stagnation.

Into this vacuum stepped a variety of evangelical parachurch, or popular religion enterprises. The Democratic nominee for the Presidency talked freely and convincingly about his born again experience. So too did the hatchetman of Watergate, Charles Colson --- both unexpected sources of endorsement from heretofore non-evangelical kinds of leaders. The searcher found the older evangelical message now being served in chic or appealing ways rather than the 'old time religion' image. For instance, Bruce Larson, a Presbyterian minister, and Keith Miller, an active layman, found a ready audience for their "relational theology". The authors recognized the need for presenting evangelical truth claims in a manner suited to the new audiences. Thus they wrote freely about putting biblical insights to work for those with sexual problems. They sensed the public's interest in personal growth and concentrated their thrust on themes such as removing guilt and anxiety, working directly at improving "inter-personal relationships", and with witnessing lovingly for the faith.[7]

Still another popular religion entrance into the revival centered on the escalating interest by the general public in the End
Times, or eschatology. Wondering whether the growing complexity
of world and national matters was not pointing to something beyond themselves, they turned by the millions to reading about the
expected imminent return of Christ to earth to destroy Satan and
reign triumphant. Since the activists of the 60s could not save this
world, perhaps Jesus was coming soon to reclaim it Himself.

Chief among this evangelical school of interpreters was Hal
Lindsey, with personal roots reaching back to the Jesus revival of
the past decade. He published in several books his conclusions that
the End Times were near, that The Late, Great Planet Earth (his
best seller) was doomed, so a seeker's only option was to prepare
himself for the coming Armageddon. One statistic makes the case.
The December 30, 1979 edition of the New York Times Book Review
stated that this title alone as at the top of the nonfiction best-
seller list; in hard cover it sold 57,227 copies, in paperback, the
total was 7,229,542. Something indeed was stirring.

Thus, to come back to an earlier point, this revival was inspired, shaped and propelled largely by the climate of opinion of
its day. It would lack the hysteria and doomsday overtones of,
say, the First or Second Great Awakenings; it had no comparable
leader as did the revivals of Dwight L. Moody or the Billy Graham
of the 1950s. Yet a revival it was, as many-sided, unsophisticated
and energetic as the American public which it served. We turn now
to examining the variety of evangelical, popular religion enterprises. Considered singly, we would not be able to claim it to be
an authentic revival. But when the important blocks are put together, they created an unmistakable edifice -- the Evangelical
Revival of the late 1970s.

CHAPTER IX

THE FAMILY AS SURVIVAL UNIT:
BILL GOTHARD AND HIS MINISTRY

The revival of the 1970s held up as its centerpiece the harvesting of souls through conversion and growth in righteousness (sanctification). To strengthen the means by which that born again life could be free to grow, evangelicals concentrated their efforts on preserving and enriching those social institutions closest to them: marriage, family, neighborhood and school, as well as one's personal devotional life. Each of the chapters in Part Three discuss one of the most influential, popular religion oriented renewal efforts.

At the core of society stood the nuclear family. Evangelicals in the 70s realized the family needed all the support it could get. Chilling evidence poured in pointing to the fact that the traditional family was rapidly losing its influence and appeal for millions of Americans. Observers could look in almost any direction and see the family in deterioration. Crimes of violence, such as assault, rape, wife and child beating increased. So too did alcoholism and drug abuse, taking their toll. Soaring rates of prostitution indicated much about the condition of marriage for some people. Organized crime helped promote easy access in pornography in books and films.

As two career families increased, so too did husbands assume greater responsibility for the children. The number of people "living together" more than doubled between 1970 and 1977. Wife swapping, singles bars and the gay option offered glamourous alternatives to traditional couples. Many who did marry chose consciously (and not by physical infertility) not to have children. And the divorce rate mounted to going over the 1 in 3 ratio by the decade's end.[1] Into this situation stepped several para-church enterprises, each aimed at protecting the family, and thus strengthening the possibilities of traditional revival breaking out.

Since much of the public interest in the evangelical revival emerges from its expert planning in public relations and image making, the phenomenal rise to great influence of the Rev. Bill Gothard should be a textbook case study on how not to succeed. He has no radio or television programs, his published writings are just now slowly appearing after many years in public ministry, he does not advertise his programs in local newspapers, he is not an especially effective speaker, he uses little psychobabble jargon, he refuses interviews about his personal life, and photographs of him are very rare (he has nothing to hide, he just doesn't like publicity). He is single, in his 40s, and lives with his parents. No beaming clan of attractive children surround him for promotion pictures -- the list of public relations omissions goes on.

But, starting in the mid-1960s, using week-long lecture series entitled "Basic Youth Conflicts" (which embraces all of religious life) he has seen attendance grow from a few hundred to where by the late 70s in cities such as St. Paul he has upwards of 30,000 in attendance. These also ignore the premises of slick public relations programs; they are hard work and cost more than a little money. Individuals pay $45 (or $35 if with an organized church group) to hear lectures on a Monday through Thursday basis, 7:00 p.m. to 10:00 p.m., with one 20 minute break; and lectures on Friday and Saturday from 9:30 a.m. to noon, 1:00 p.m. to 4:30 p.m. and 6:30 p.m. to 9:30 p.m. Further, no small group or "buzz sessions" are held for group discussions. It is all lecturing, all following a very large loose-leaf manual with printed materials to which additional handouts are embedded at each session.

Those in attendance take notes and keep coming back in larger numbers each year, bringing friends and taking notes on the new materials being added to the basic lectures. Gothard lectures live about half of these; the other half being done by videotape. Yet without the promotional techniques of other leaders, Gothard has more than durability and tight organization to offer the crowds. His program is an excellent example of an evangelical holding fast to traditional verities and being accepted by large audiences who find in his messages the authority renewal to hold fast in a world coming apart.

Critics and friends agree his strength is in his ability to demonstrate in unusually precise, well organized practical form, a system of biblical answers to the questions he knows are worrying his audiences. He assumes that the Bible, word for word, was known in the mind of God before it was given to mankind; it needed not one word more or less. Everything in it fits together in logical, harmonious balance; it is perfectly planned and expressed. When one is receptive to this idea of a prehistorical plan underlying the scriptures, he or she can more easily understand God has a concrete, immediately applicable answer to the seeker's specific question.

Further, Gothard's presentation leaves little room for doubts, fear, or uncertainties. His own quiet demeanor, modest lifestyle, and lack of razzle dazzle, combined with the Institute as presenting the Bible as Answer Book, convinces his audiences that evangelical Christianity in America is still sound at heart since it can produce so remarkable a spokesman as this. In brief, if one can accept his conviction of the inerrancy and verbal inspiration and uncomplicated unity of the Bible, that person is open to the ministry of Bill Gothard. [2]

As is the case with many other evangelical spokesmen, Gothard presents in his lectures a combination of scriptural proof texts, psychology, common sense, anecdotes about personal triumphs over adversity and inspiration (but no references to, say,

Luther, Calvin or Wesley). The standard program (it is not a "seminar" as advertised since the seminar format is not used) has con-
sisted to date of lectures on: self image (acceptance of self);
family (communication breakdown, chain of command); conscience
(removing guilt, gaining a clear conscience); rights (turning bit-
terness into forgiveness, transforming irritations, yielding personal
rights); freedom (moral freedom, increasing sensitivity, cycles of
life); success (successful living); purpose (eight qualities essen-
tial in success, eight callings in discovering life purpose); friends
(friendship); dating (successful dating patterns); and commitment
(life in a new dimension).

This program rests on an extremely carefully reasoned progression. From a better understanding of one's self, one moves out
to improving family relations, coming to grips with sin in the form
of guilt in interpersonal relations, maintaining one's individuality
in a society of conflicting claims, opportunities for personal growth
under the will of God; learning to know how one is measuring up
(i.e., "success"); and in the last sessions what the majority of
the audiences are the most interested in; how to cope with family,
courting and marriage problems, and what to expect from this in
one's new life.

Interestingly, Gothard assumes, as most other evangelists do
not, that the born again experience, whether it be gradual or in-
stantaneous, is something the listeners understand, and probably
have experienced. What Gothard seeks to do is rekindle older commitments -- or decisions -- for Christ, tie together loose ends among
those seeking a precise understanding of the Bible's message for
them, and introduce younger listeners to this interpretation of the
Christian life.

The above schedule is for the basic class; advanced sessions
are given for veteran listeners and for ministers. In each case,
following the tradition of lecturers such as Norman Vincent Peale,
Gothard uses in the handouts and on the overhead projector a
series of groupings such as "4 levels of conflict," "6 problems in

gaining forgiveness," or "3 steps in transforming irritation." These are given as authoritative statements, not theses to be debated. The listener thus tests his or her own state of mind or moral condition against these norms, making a diagnosis and then awaiting Gothard's answer. That is invariably supported by numerous Bible verses, creating an atmosphere of authority, being fully in harmony with the will of God.

Since it would be impossible to summarize the major teachings of the week's seminar (Bockelman's analysis includes four topics) I will look at another one, germane to the theme of this book.

Given the crisis of the sexual revolution, Gothard and his audience are deeply concerned about reversing it, or slowing it down and in finding their own Bible-found pilgrimage through today's moral wasteland. The lecturer thus gives detailed attention to "Moral Freedom" and his teaching establishes authority, holds on to older truths, concentrates on inner concerns and stands or falls on the basis of his interpretations and arrangements of Bible verses.

Definitions are the starting point; the opposite of "freedom" is "bondage" to that which keeps the believer from a full Christian life. Gothard defines and uses brief texts to indentify 7 forms of bondage: lasciviousness, sensuality, concupiscence, defrauding, reprobation, fornication, and freedom in sex (or sexual liberty). With his form of exegesis, the Bible has a firm statement to make on each -- Gothard's pattern is superimposed over the writings of the biblical authors.

That established, the audience learns the visible symptoms of bondage -- or moral conflict of those whose action conflicts with the will of God. Gothard lists six such symptoms: resentment toward life, a sensual attitude, moral argumentation, doctrinal argumentation, contempt for divine authority, and rejection of eternal punishment or reward. Each of these is also supported by a New Testament proof text.

Then the student learns the discerning evidences of moral conflict by studying Gothard's charts of behavioral patterns of inner

motivation. Three such patterns exist: that of God's, that of society
and that which rejects all standards (the latter two being tied
back to the 7 forms of bondage. The message here is that as sin-
ners we cannot help violating our God-given freedom, but we must
find balance and freedom so as to live under God's rules and standards.

For those who might not be aware of how such departures develop, Gothard explains, by way of example, the six forms in which
lasciviousness may emerge, using Old and New Testament support,
and how the same trouble over the emergence of concupiscence can
develop. In both cases the trouble starts when the seeker ignores
the basic ground rules God has established so as to lead him to
authentic freedom.

Once, however, the seeker understands the dangers of one or
more of the seven forms of bondage, he is at least started on the
way towards moral freedom, victory over those forces which plague
America today. From II Peter 1:5-10 Gothard draws eight qualities
which turn around the believer from bondage to victory: faith,
purity, knowledge, self control, endurance, godliness, sensitivity
and love. Using real life situations to illustrate his point, he
drives home the point that one might well control the symptoms of
lasciviousness or the others, but the true believer must seek to
eliminate the cause, not just the symptom. The real, final enemy
here becomes pride, one's refusal to honor God as God.

Here the heart of Godhard's argument on this topic is
reached. He approvingly quotes a passage from a book by Wesley
Nelson Captivated By Christ, stating that "God and man cannot be
reconciled simply by God being gracious and loving enough to overlook our faults and forgive our sins. Release must be something
more than ordinary forgiveness. It must be something which will
redeem us from the power of sin so that God may again become God
in us."[3] The scriptural authority for this release is James 4:7-10
about humility and mourning before God restores the penitent. The
implication here (to this author) is the tendency towards triumph-
alism; once released, the believer can -- and probably will -- lead

a triumphant spiritual life over sin when still on this earth. Here law triumphs over grace, an issue much in dispute among Christians. The use of the Book of James with its emphasis on good works bears out the contention that sin, or bondage, is masterable in this life. Gothard concludes by showing how once the humiliation and release have occurred, the Christian grows in moral freedom.

The believer keeps in spiritual conditioning through the program the lecturer then establishes for the new life. She or he starts by rebuilding one's thoughts, goals and emotions; memorizing scripture, revising personal goals to eliminate pride and daring to live the new, released life. God works through this pattern. One is to think thoughts about God, welcome tests of one's faith, expose experiences to the criteria of God's truth, believe God's word is the final truth and thus know the power that one has, released, and able to drive away wrong thoughts.

Moral freedom is within the grasp of those who follow this program. Recognize evil for what it is, learn to hate it, be ready to test temptation because it can be overcome; then learn to walk in the Spirit of God by taking in His word, testing His thoughts, resisting evil and allowing one's self to mature and to minister to others. All this creates a spiritual pattern, a rhythm or tempo in one's spiritual life. By recognizing it, we are able to resist evil and do what is right. This is moral freedom.

Gothard obviously attracts critics as well as supporters. Some wonder about his empirical evidence for teaching Divine Order without his being married or a parent; others wonder how directly in touch he is with teenagers other than those who attend his meetings. Gothard himself informs potential (and published) critics that public evaluation of ministries such as his are probably not biblical. He cites Matthew 18:15 to show that public critical examination is not God's way; two Christians who disagree should talk over the matter in private. By so doing, his closest watcher notes, Gothard believes any differences could be resolved and thus avoid

public criticism of the Institute. This attitude illustrates Gothard's
deeply felt belief that for every situation in life, one can find a
precisely applicable answer in the Bible.

It is that conviction of his, perhaps more than any other,
that brings on the criticism from outsiders. Gothard leaves little
room for ambiguity, for the mysteries seen through the glass
darkly, for the obvious tensions between authors or positions in
the Bible, for doubting that an immediately applicable Bible verse
is not available for life's situations.[5]

Martin Marty, like Bockelman, is impressed with the enormous
enthusiasm among church goers for Gothard and for some of his
teachings. Yet to Marty the answers are too tidy, too neat and too
authoritarian. One finds little room for the surprises of grace, the
serendipity God has in store for those without following a step by
step program towards overcoming sin. Like other preachers on authority of the 1970s, Gothard makes life's struggles over evil too
simple because the Bible is made to appear other than what it is
(not a perfectly designed jigsaw puzzle). Finally, to Marty, the
tendency in Basic Youth Conflicts is towards excessive inward con-
templation, which is in harmony with the ME Decade theme, but
lacks a spontaneous social outreach towards the oppressed.[6]

Another observer found too little room for failure in Gothard's
explanations; failure is more than personal, its mastery requires
more than wholesomethinking. Perhaps the formula which pointed
to avoidance of failure is what is at fault.[7]

Finally, the Bishop of an American Lutheran Church district
finds Gothard appeals to the lonely, those lacking in intimacy in
a depersonalized society. They need "signs and wonders" as alternatives to "faith, trust, love and mystery." Believing this world
is coming apart, they accept those who preach with authority on
"other-worldly simplicities". The world that Gothard talks about
need not be, this critic writes. The institutional church can be
made to vibrate "with the freedom that is found in Christ." That
is achieved by sound exegetical preaching and teaching; prophetic

and insightful understanding of our times; admission of one's failures and defeats, but also a recognition that no formula can encapsulate the freedom and release found in the living Word.[8]

Gothard also comes under criticism from those evangelicals (see pp. 55-9) who do not share his inerrancy views on the Bible. Since his ministry is still very much intact, it is too early to make any final assessment of his place in the evangelical revival. That movement's first historian, Richard Quebedeaux, considers him a highly successful popularizer, important because he can attract and hold so many thousands of people and provide them with what they do not hear in their own congregations.[9]

During the summer of 1980 Basic Youth Conflicts Institute underwent a profound shake-up in leadership. After disclosure that Bill Gothard's brother Steve, administrator of the daily activities of the Institute, confessed to "deception and fornication with several women," Steve resigned from the organization, and Bill and his father resigned from the board of directors. Bill Gothard himself greatly reduced his personal appearances in seminar institutes. Yet, with the matter publically aired, the first steps towards restoring public confidence in the program had been taken. The Institute continued its scheduled activities largely by means of videotape. Bill stated in his disclosure letter "I ask for your prayers for my family, staff and their families, the board and me at this time...."[10]

CHAPTER X

Marabelle Morgan: An Evangelical Pressing On

Some readers may think it a joke, or in poor taste, that the chapter on Marabelle Morgan follows directly after Bill Gothard. The differences in lifestyle, in tone and sales promotion techniques within evangelicalism today could hardly be greater than exists between these two. Morgan has been the cover story on Time, interviewed on the major television talk shows, and speaks freely and openly about intimate matters of her life, and has no aversion to having her picture associated with her product, namely "The Total Woman." Yet both she and Gothard influence millions of readers and listeners; both clearly fit within the evangelical boundaries. Apparently one has to have lived in the United States during these past years to understand why I can make that statement. When I presented my preliminary findings on this subject to a group of American and British church women who were long-time residents of Chiengmai, Thailand, knowing of Morgan only through the Asian editions of Time and Newsweek, they simply could not understand!

But the lighter vein in which Morgan is studied, by comparison to other option shaping evangelicals, is necessary to establish because she brings the message that sexual intimacy within marriage is not only a blessing of God, but it is fun, real fun. Some evangelicals and others have trouble with that exuberance. But we will discuss the critics later. For the moment we can say that among the dozens of books, many by born again believers, on sexual identity and behavior published in this age, none has outsold

or attracted more imitators than Morgan's <u>Total Woman</u> and <u>Total</u>
<u>Joy</u>. Whatever one may think of her message, there are millions of
customers who buy it.

In brief summary, the Morgan phenomenon is both a culmination and a beginning for evangelicals. Her understanding of hus-
band/wife relationships is identified with that of Larry Christenson,
Bill Gothard and the submission school; in that sense her ideas are
a culmination. But they are a beginning also because her books
talk so freely, often in a risqué manner about techniques for sexual stimulation and intimacy that it can only be dubbed innovative
(not for long-time students of the subject, but for evangelicals).
What the Morgan books, and the hundreds of short-course training
sessions led by Morgan-trained directors across the country, mostly
in churches, accomplished was in offering biblical authority, plus
no-nonsense biological instruction for which married couples were
searching in the 70s. The Morgan program told them it was OK to
enjoy intimacy, to make it fun, to work at improving it, and (since
dozens of other manuals had the same message) to believe this was
God's will for them. A part of the ME Decade, they accepted the
situation that since they couldn't improve the world, they could
at least improve their own lives.

Yet beneath all this fun-and-games veneer rests some very
important questions and doubts about the program itself. It uti-
lizes the most sophisticated marketing techniques for its market in
mass distribution today. A customer at a bookstore can purchase
along with the Morgan books, a tape cassette with more instructions, all gracefully packaged in blushing pink on the display kit.
What this, and the Total Woman seminars, so popular in all parts
of the country suggest, is that someone in the TW team understood
a potential market and built on it.

By 1974 when the first book came out, the counteroffensive
by evangelical and other women against the sexual revolution was
growing strongly. They recognized the threat to the family with
liberalized divorce laws, public laxity about 'living together',

books about 'open marriage', demands for childrens' day care centers, and the often shrill rhetoric of the anti-male liberationists
all coalesced to convince many women the American family needed
to be saved.[1] To help them do that, many of the women's magazines
gradually but firmly started to project women in stories and advertising as inherently sexy, irresistible to one's man if only this
or that product were used. Make-up and cosmetics used once only
by show business girls became everyday fare in retail stores. Mag-
zines and books "were all too ready to present instructions...or
how to maximize sexual pleasure." One further example helps make
the point. By the magic of television, and the all-American pen-
chant to be No. 1 in competition, many evangelicals by now had
reversed their long-standing disdain for beauty pageants; now they
welcomed the testimony-giving winners and held them up to their
own daughters as role models.[2]

Beyond that, as the writers of the Time cover story on Morgan
suggested, many couples never came to experience the good times
or happiness promised by the marriage manuals and the self improvement hucksters. Most of them were hassled by inflation, inadequate housing, conflicting advice about childrearing, guilt feelings
about variety in sexual expression, an inability to obtain a college
education with its built-in upward mobility, and unwilling to com-
pete in the world of factories or offices. Unable to control the
larger world, they could provide security and love for their husbands and families. Most of them took their religion seriously, and
needed direction for finding some happiness since the glamour alternatives shown them in the mass media were beyond their reach.[3]

Many of them settled for the Total Woman program of
Marabelle Morgan. After a year and a half study at Ohio State University, she had become a beautician, "there with the water running, I was born again. I had always been fascinated by God, but
I had talked to Him and had never got any answers. This time I
asked Him to take me and He took me. There was no bolt of light-
ening, only peace. I was tickled to death."[4]

After joining Campus Crusade for Christ as a fulltime worker, she met and soon married law student Charles Morgan. Children soon came, as did conversations with wives of the Miami Dolphin football players, study of the Bible, and readings in Ann Landers and Dale Carnegie. From this emerged the ideas that came to be Total Woman in 1974. To everyone's surprise it caught on quickly and moved to the top of the best seller lists and stayed there. In fact, the New York Times survey found that book to be the ninth best seller of the 70s in non-fiction with some 903,000 hard cover and 2,700,000 paperback books sold.

Through her writings, seminars, and television appearances Morgan's name had become a household word. The most talked about feature of her program has been her explicit advice on how to arouse one's husband's sexual interests; the author describes how costumes, candlelight dinners, long weekends, and bubble baths among other suggestions are recommended and required homework for those in the seminars. Her recommendations result directly from her concept of the wife being in submission to her husband, to adapt to his interests, to be what he wants her to be. Morgan writes that this is part of God's plan and the wife's responsibility to God and to her husband. The Morgan family has daily Bible study and meditation as part of its religious growth. They found, for instance, direction in implementing what the Bible states "...let her breasts satisfy thee at all times; and be thou ravished with her love." [5]

She found other scripture (e.g., Rom. 5:12; Psalms 51:11) which she originally thought meant that sex was sinful. She found instead that God had meant that sex was for the pleasure of the married couples. The key verse in her system is "Marriage is honorable in all, and the bed undefiled: (Heb. 13:4 KJV). She explains, "In other words, sex is for the marriage relationship only, but within those bounds, anything goes. Sex is as clean and pure as eating cottage cheese." [6]

Morgan's inner faith has given her abundant life; peace with God, pardon from sins, purpose in life, power to love and to transform. The need is there, the authority for such an outlook is there, the opportunity is there to be a Total Woman. She concludes Total Joy with "Ladies, start your engines."[7]

The books contain much practical, common sense advice on housekeeping, childrearing, budget management, weight control and the like. Thus, in some respects, the structure of Total Woman and Total Joy is close to Gothard's; clear diagnosis of the problem (sin reigns when one is apart from God); the rewards of the transformed life are available (the born again experience). In both instances, both authors present orderly, one-two-three step programs towards achieving both short and long term goals. The major difference between the two being, obviously, the openness with which each discusses the sexual relationship between husband and wife.

Beyond that, Morgan relies on a different style of motivation than Gothard to change behavior. The latter relies often on fear of God's punishment, while Morgan appeals to the "Four A's"; accept your husband as he is; admire your husband every day; adapt to his way of life; and appreciate all he does for you. She also suggests that not only will this make the husband a better provider, lover and friend, but also will lead him to bring home gifts for her rather than problems from the office. The books and Total Woman seminars are replete with stories about happy husbands coming home with flowers, candy or lingerie to their revitalized wives. Morgan's husband, in fact, brought her a new refrigerator-freezer. To her this is not manipulation, it is offering women hope for their marriages.[8]

However, many evangelicals and other believe that such behavior hardly befits those claiming the born again experience. Jim Wallis, leader of the discipleship community in Washington, D.C., named the Sojourners, writes:

Marabelle Morgan has a new message for evangelical women, so long cloistered and told that sex was dirty.

Now they can be "total women" who are successful sex symbols and skillful manipulators of male ego, all under the guise of wifely submissiveness to husbands and justified in the name of Christian principles. Evangelical wives and single women can now look like Hollywood starlets and feel good about it. No more fundamentalist prohibitionists against make-up, fashionable wardrobes or sexy outfits.[9]

To Wallis, and others, the Morgan followers have sold out to society's definition of success, fame, and popularity. Other evangelicals, such as Patricia Gundry, object strongly to the position that men have all the rights, and women have all the responsibilities. They are in fact second class citizens, able to function only as servants and stereotyped sex objects for their husbands.[10]

Peggy Noll calls "Total Woman" a caricature. It implies a single woman cannot be a whole woman. It is not selfless love but given so that the husband will start bringing home those extras the wife has wanted. To Noll, Morgan quotes the Bible when it suits her purpose but the argument is simplistic and self-serving. Noll recommends the book not be read.[11] Mainline churches such as the United Methodists have developed full critiques of it. Feminists outside church circles have been equally denunciatory, the most penetrating being perhaps that of Joyce Maynard: "The image of women presented in TW is an ultimately demeaning one, and it demeans men as well; it represents women as weak and empty-headed complainers, obsessed with material possessions. I do not like to think what would happen to a Total Woman if her husband died."[12]

Yet almost everyone agrees that at least Morgan helped bring sex out of the closet (literally, in the case of the woman married for years who still changed into her nightwear in her closet); it taught the reader not to use sex as a punishment, or to ignore the good signs and feelings the body can give. Among other evangelicals, John Scanzoni condemns the technique of the TW wife greeting the husband home from work clad only in apron and black stockings; this done not to interject new life in the marriage, but really

to make him pliable to her controls. "Shades of Samson and
Delilah!" he wrote, "What hypocrisy -- telling a wife she is subject to her husband and then encouraging her to use sex to mani-
pulate him." Evangelical criticism of Morgan is not only sarcastic.
Scanzoni argues for assertiveness, not submission, in wives. That
means "to determine what one should or must do because it is
right in the sight of God and because it is fair and just to oneself
and to others, and then to act on those convictions."[13]

Other evangelicals are concerned with improving sexual iden-
tity without docility. Among the more insightful works here are
Bruce Larson and Keith Miller, Living the Adventure, Tim and
Beverly La Haye, The Act of Marriage and Lewis Smedes, Sex for
Christians. These authors often do not agree, but the themes they
share in common are far more numerous and important.

Among these writers the question of authority and submission
has been replaced by mutuality; an acceptance of each other's roles
in the world, and a mutual sharing and decision making process
for the issues of the marriage, family and the household. These
authors believe that the sexual act itself is fulfilling only when
complete concern for the other is expressed; where power games are
left behind and where full attention to the needs of the other are
faced, hence the need for full time mutuality.

These evangelicals agree with Morgan that the sexual experience for Christians is healthy and a blessing; they cite polls showing Christian women enjoying sex as much if not more than the un-
committed. They also insist on the element of full concern and responsibility for the welfare of the spouse; women are, in other
words, more than sex objects, playmates, potential or actual
mothers and housekeepers. Further, they suggest, some women may
well demonstrate traditionally "masculine traits" some may be "basi-
cally aggressive, competent managers and organizers" and should
not be made to feel less feminine for that. Role playing is rejected in favor of full and open commitment and communication.
Problems of child discipline should be given the same amount of

seriousness as a crisis at one's profession. And willingness or re-servations about the sexual act on a given evening should be freely discussed rather than repressed or sublimated in the name of sub-mission.[14]

In conclusion, one must be careful not to draw overly sharp lines among evangelical opinion makers on the matters of sexual identity in marriage. Nor must one assume evangelicals as a whole have different desires, fantasies or interests than the general popu-lation. What has not yet been resolved in the evangelical commun-ity (or elsewhere) is the extent to which traditional norms, so deeply ingrained in childhood, should be held fast, while the cur-rent social norms tell us to press forth with all deliberate speed.

CHAPTER XI

PRESERVING THE FAITH:
THE BOOM IN THE CHRISTIAN SCHOOL MOVEMENT

The evangelical revival receives much of its grassroots support in the rapidly growing Christian School movement. While Roman Catholics and some Lutheran and Anabaptist bodies have operated primary and secondary schools for decades, the evangelicals in the past decade have been adding thousands of independent, theologically conservative schools in all parts of the nation. The best total estimate is that by early 1978 some 5,000 such schools enrolling close to 1,000,000 students are in operation; this means about 1 out of 10 American children is in some kind of church related school.[1]

This expansion can be traced back to the same general set of causes that gave birth to the born again crusade in our day: a sharply declining lack of confidence in a basic American institution -- the public school; a realization that reform on a national scale is impossible, hence (like improving the family or marriage or one's self) working for change at the closest point to home; a recognition of the common enemy, here the secularist spirit in public education; and an overwhelming desire by parents to reestablish among youth a sense of permanent authority before they enter a world of bewildering choices and enticing alternative lifestyles made glamorous by the mass media. In brief, one cannot find a better case study of evangelical revival than in the Christian School movement; the basic ingredients are there.

Yet, we should note here some difficulties in studying the movement. The Christian schools pride themselves on their independence from strict public control. This shows up in their independence from cooperating often with one another in more than a minimal way, and also frustrates any efforts of those seeking precise information about enrollment patterns. Finally, my study makes no claim at comprehensive coverage since in several cases my requests for information were not met. Hopefully someone today is doing a comprehensive history of the movement.

Lacking a central information center, we must draw from a variety of sources; first, the number of students involved; second, the philosophy and goals of the movement; third, the methods and curriculum utilized; and finally, in this book a case study of how one organization within the movement operates since its influence is strong enough to warrant such a detailed look.

The Christian School movement is organized loosely into four national organizations, each with its own curricular guides, hiring and administrative practices, and unique religious priorities. These are: (1) The National Association of Christian Schools, a part of the National Association of Evangelicals, with headquarters in Wheaton, Illinois and enrolling some 30,300 students, 2,100 teachers, and 30 years in operation; (2) The National Union of Christian Schools, operating out of Grand Rapids, Michigan, with 304 schools, 62,269 students, 3,500 teachers and some fifty years of experience in teaching; (3) the newly federated Association of Christian Schools, International has its center in Whittier, California, with some 50,000 students, 3,175 teachers and 5 years of operational history; and (4) The American Association of Christian Schools, with 650 member institutions and nearly 90,000 students, is headquartered in Normal, Illinois.[2]

Beyond these, and at times working independently, are several regional associations, such as the Mid-Atlantic Christian School Association, the Great Plains Association, Texas Organization, New England Association and more. Some, such as the well known Christian Liberty Academy of Suburban Chicago, operate independently from an association. Others, such as the Christian Lights Association of Harrisonburg, Virginia, affiliated with the Mennonites, encourage concerned parents to start their own schools and offer a complete portfolio for that purpose. Whatever the grand total amounts to, the movement is very popular, is growing, and will probably be the principle agency of the evangelical revival today to keep it functioning well into the future.

Among the many statements of the philosophy and goals of the movement available for a case study here, we examine an article by Prof. Nicholas Wolterstorff of Calvin College.[3] The writings of Dr. Frank Gaebelein are also a major source for extended consideration.

Wolterstorff accepts the pluralistic nature of American society and the benefits of religious diversity. Within that, the public school movement functions along what he calls the "common-denominator" method; outside the domains of church and family, American organizations unite on what they hold in common, regardless of their particular denomination. Americans have not tried to secularize public life, only to remove "sectarian" tendencies and search for common components. This leads to the escalating degree of secularism in American public institutions, including the schools. The author finds "a vapid secularism combined with a firm though ungrounded insistence on the importance of man" as the dominant scene in public educational philosophy.[4]

Some religious bodies, such as Roman Catholic, Lutherans and Calvinists have dissented from this common denominator view and have placed in their schools a study of "The God who is at the center of the Redeemer who works out His redemption centrally in Jesus Christ." Any educational practice that splits life into parts and ignores that center is inadequate.

With the rampant secularism in public schools, these dissenters and others interested in Christian education are now asking for a change in the structure of American education. "We are asking that we no longer be relegated to the position of dissenters." This statement is the key to the entire movement. What the author, and indeed most leaders in the movement want is that "the distribution of funds for education be education-blind."[5] Acknowledging that much of the general public deeply fears the use of tax revenue for sectarian schools, the author points out the Christian school spokesmen want an integrated education. That includes instruction in "responsible loyalty to the nation." It also means they want an integrated education, one which "must display signs of the kingdom of God's love."[6] This combination, loyalty to the nation and religious underpinning, can best be met in the Christian school which maintains the highest academic standards, in which the students are taught they have responsibilities for participation in American society. They are to be trained "to live within American society, working for the fulfillment of its people." The standard for measurement is "God's standard of how devotedly they worship and praise God himself, how tenderly they care for the plants and the animals, and how lovingly they work for the liberation and fulfillment of all humanity."[7] In brief, the Christian school can produce graduates "filled with the gentle but all-conquering love of Jesus Christ...who are restlessly discontent with things as they are, and ever pushing forward to the new age."[8] That is a marvelous synthesis of holding fast and pressing on.

A very wide variety of specific curriculum materials is available for the schools, a situation highly encouraging to the leaders since this means they rather than some state board of education can select classroom items. Many schools utilize the 1890's McGuffy Readers as their introduction to reading, preferring the strict memorization and moral lessons found there to the more recent materials. Many Christian schools use self-paced systems where the daily schedule works something like this: After opening exercises each student works during the morning by himself or herself in self-taught programs, progressing at their own speed on a given subject. The teacher is available for assistance but not for repetitive drill. The afternoons are given to more traditional forms, such as discussions, lectures and group projects. Most schools avoid what they consider "frills"; driver education, manual arts courses or drama, for example. They concentrate on the skills of reading, writing and arithmetic, plus penmanship, heavy emphasis on Bible study and occasionally some Greek in high schools. Throughout the emphasis is on discipline and respect for authority.

Special attention at all levels is given to inculcating the literal interpretation of the Genesis account of creation. The curriculums are unanimous in believing any use of the logic of evolutionary thought is extremely dangerous. Equally strong attention is given at each age level to carefully prepared courses in doctrine, history and hymnology.

Friends and critics alike agree many of these schools a decade or so ago were started to keep white children from having to integrate in the public schools with Blacks or other ethnic minorities. And to this day few of those minorities are found in these classrooms. Yet the largest increase in enrollment has come in the last 3 to 5 years, when fears of desegregation were decreasing, but fears of a new subversion, this known as "secular humanism" helped bring tens of thousands of children to these institutions.[9] Some interpreters, such as Schafly, find a unified conspiracy here to destroy the fabric of American society: ERA, abortion, gay rights, the women's movement, secular humanism -- all are combined to create a deadly threat to the survival of America.

The evangelical community is sharply divided over the extent to which any such conspiracy exists. Few parents are willing to acknowledge publically what they intuitively believe to be true -- the presence of the secular humanism philosophy which will corrupt America. While the major periodicals of evangelicalism such as Christianity Today, Eternity, Christian Life and others have not given the topic any notice, several small, less known evangelical groups have emerged in recent years furnishing the targets and the remedies for the crisis in the schools. The best known of these are: The Barbara M. Morris Report of Ellicott City, Maryland; Christian Family Renewal of Clovis, California; and The Heritage Foundation of Washington, DC.

They find in secular humanism the enemy the staunch conservatives of the 1950s found in political and religious liberalism -- the means by which the sacred elements in American life created by God are being undermined; what is wrong with America today is traceable to secular humanism. Instead of inculcating respect for the basic skills of reading and writing, instead of teaching right from wrong, today's educators are instead letting children decide for themselves what to learn and what to believe. In brief, America is coming apart when its prime resource, its children, are taught that truth and ethics are relative, that values and moral judgments are situational, that whatever the secular world holds up as "fun" is good, be that gay rights, pornography, rock music, promiscuity, whatever makes one feel good. Such is the indictment of secular humanism.[10]

Such is the case for Christian schools and against public schools. To bring the crusade to the grassroots, organizations such as Christian Family Renewal of Clovis, California, have emerged in recent years; this we will look at as a case study of one organization in the field. This organization recognizes that not all concerned parents will be able to afford to send their children to private Christian schools, or have the opportunity to do so. Thus the task is to give the parents information about how secular humanism is corrupting their children, what other communities are doing about it, and what one's efforts can do to restore Christian morality and decency to our way of life again.

The leader is Dr. Murray Norris, a one time writer, who in the early 1970s was devoted full time to building and expanding Christian Family Renewal -- a lecture and information service. He has been spending most of his time in smaller towns working with parents on how to convince local school boards what secular humanism has been doing to their curriculums and what everyone together can do to correct it. His agency provides tapes, pamphlets and other materials on rock music, gays, religious cults, pornography, sex education -- almost the entire gamut of concerns raised by the sexual revolution of the 1970s.

I learned about this program by reading a printed advertisement giving details about the appearance of Dr. Norris in my former community, Burnsville, Minnesota, on April 15, 1978. The advertisement stated Norris " is currently a member of the faculty of St. John's University, Collegeville, Minnesota." The ad also mentioned he was President of Valley Christian University in California and holder of a law degree. I attended the meeting, a rather low-key lecture on the impact of secular humanism in the public schools before an audience of some 200, all of whom seemed to be in the age group of parents of public school children. No hard sell or undue emotional tone was apparent.

However, a reporter for the weekly hometown Burnsville Current investigated Dr. Norris' credentials more extensively. He was told by St. John's University that Norris was not presently and has never been a member of that school's faculty. Norris served as an instructor in a short summer program conducted on that campus under the supervision of the university's Human Life program. The university officials told the reporter it would be "wrong for Norris to identify himself as connected in any way with St. John's." When the reporter asked about Valley Christian University, it was learned from Mrs. Norris by telephone conversation that the school was "just barely starting and very small. It's for people who are working and who want to get a college degree wherever they are." No students were enrolled at that time. [11]

Morris replied in the Current that he did not teach during the regular sessions at St. John's. "I mentioned during the talk that I had only taught there a single week each year. Do you find something wrong with this?" (That information was not on the promotional flyer.) As to Valley Christian University, he stated it is a subsidiary of Christian Family Renewal. It had "received its approval from the State of California, Department of Education on August 29, 1977. We had no students at all during 1977. We started accepting students early this year." Norris suggested the reporter would have received more accurate information by talking with the Registrar rather than Mrs. Norris. The Current reporter responded that after rechecking all the information, he had no reason to change his reportage.[12]

This rather small scale incident is discussed here in considering the evangelical resurgence because it is a good example of how a considerable amount of information about issues as crucial as public school curricula gets into the hands of the general public, and how difficult it is for parents and administrators to know the sources of charges made against the schools. The tendency, as we have seen, today is to suspect institutions and their leaders, not the least being public school officials. Information such as provided by organizations as mentioned here tend frequently to polarize rather than clarify the problems facing parents, students and the school officials. The best of the Christian School movement, that which follows the ideals set down by Prof. Wolterstorff, for instance, suggests the constructive alternatives that the crusade can offer. Other organizations under the evangelical umbrella may well raise critical problems for those unable to participate directly in the Christian School movement, but not furnish answers the entire community can live with over a long period of time.

In summary, the Christian School movement in all of its variety offers a panoramic view of the diversity of the evangelical revival itself. Its vision, and often its expression, reflects the best of the concern by parents for the future of their families and the society at large. But, the opportunities for oversimplification and motivating parents by fear more than by accurate information is a risk everyone concerned has yet to understand.

CHAPTER XII

REVIVAL ACROSS THE LAND:
THE POPULAR RELIGION OF HOLDING FAST

Beyond the rapidly growing popularity of the Schlaflys, Gothards, Morgans and the Christian School movement, the revival of 1976–80 made its presence known in an unprecedented way through the medium of the mass media. There the holders fast reached untold millions of Americans, demonstrating its strength, adaptability and leadership for the demands of popular religion. Here the holders fast controlled the message of revival in a convincing manner. In talking to a mass audience they could ignore the complexities of argument and documentation demanded by the pressers on. They held fast to the traditional evangelical demand for instant conversion, a personal relationship with Jesus as one's Lord and Savior, and the need to share that good news as widely as possible. In brief, the revival showed its clout and its personality the most convincingly on the popular level.

Evangelical leaders, long awaiting signs of revival, hailed its appearance with bold enthusiasm. Their unofficial historian went so far as to say that "evangelicalism, in its Protestant, Catholic and charismatic forms, is really the mainstream brand of American Christianity."[1] George Gallup, Jr., called the Bicentennial year "The Year of the Evangelical," an assessment seconded by Christianity Today, U.S. News and World Report and Newsweek; the outpouring was made the feature story of the Christmas issue for 1976 of Time. Careful students of the religious scene such as Garry

Wills and Michael Novak expressed admiration for the strength and vitality of the revival. Leaders of the National Association of Evangelicals hailed it as "the most significant religious movement of this half of the century."[2]

To be sure, the depth and extent of revivals in America have become increasingly difficult to measure; an upsurge is not a true revival simply because the individuals and publications say it is. As revivals grow in size and scope out of small community events, so too does the accuracy of measuring their impact.[3] The firm evidence at hand today comes from several inter-related sources; the boom in religious publishing, the acceleration in religious television and radio programming, and the fantastic appeal of the born again celebrity. All of these are far removed from the revival days of a Jonathan Edwards or Charles G. Finney. Yet they are the artifacts of our time, not a bygone era, and are the materials we have now for our evaluation.

Many of the more traditional signs of revival are also present in our day; when added together they do present a convincing case. For instance, church attendance, at its lowest point in 1974 in 20 years, started a small upturn. Enrollments in evangelical seminaries show a gradual increase. Some observers reported a rapid growth in private and group Bible study groups "now attracting 1 out of every 5 Americans each week by some estimates."[4] Martin Marty, in reviewing the unofficial history of the outbreak, found it most profoundly expressed among the millions of "otherworldly" Appalachian poor and ghetto Blacks, among believers who "gather in storefronts or little frame churches on windswept Texas hills...." He hails "evangelical young and old who grieve over the behavioral shift...," those who go to "the prisons and homes for senior citizens, in vigil at the side of alcoholic spouses, in prayer on beds of terminal illness, the ugly and crippled and impotent...."[5] A sizeable number of evangelical communities was created in cities and towns in every part of the nation. Evangelicals became involved as never before in community renewal and improving race relations.

But it is impossible to document these; hence they are listed here
as an integral part of the revival, but without formal proof.[6]

Another deviation from older revivals was the failure of the
new born again to separate into new denominations. Some individual congregations or portions of them undoubtedly did so, but we
have no way of measuring such change. Rather today's revival
shows a marked trend towards continuing one's denominational loyalty, and support for the many attractive para-church programs.

Convincing evidence does appear, however, in publishing, the
"electronic" church, and the celebrities and to those we now turn.
One underlying question must be raised here before continuing. We
may well ask: Just because of the boom in evangelical book sales
or the electronic church or the enthusiasm for born again celebrity
speakers, does that really signify a revival? What measurable data
exists that people's lives were turned around into evangelical
channels? The answer must lie in looking briefly at the assumptions behind the use of those data. The assumption used by this
author is that people will not spend time and money on books or
television revivalists or turn out in large numbers for revival meetings over a period of years unless they believed some needs were
being met by such behavior. All of these activities are voluntary
in nature; hence, the choice of evangelical expressions was the result of a decision made by each person involved. Granted that the
successful revivalists used advertising 'hidden persuaders' and
bandwagon motivation, yet the time and money invested is convincing.

Starting in the mid-70s, an enormous increase of sales of
evangelical, revivalist subjects spread over the publishing world,
quite unparalleled in American history. In 1976, sales of religious
books (mostly born again, but exclusive of Bibles and hymnals)
jumped 24 per cent over 1975. One cautious estimate placed religious
book sales at over a half billion dollars, or about 15 per cent of
the total book industry. Among the best sellers (besides Marabelle
Morgan and Hal Lindsey, see pp. 88, 98) were works by Billy

Graham, Charles Colson (Born Again), Ruth Carter Stapleton, Tim
and Beverly Le Haye, Larry Christenson and Johnny Cash. Titles of
best sellers from lesser known authors reflected the growing interest
in marriage, childrearing and subjects like You Can Be the Wife
of a Happy Husband.[7]

Religious booksellers discovered that supermarkets, drugstores,
and other commercial outlets catering to family trade (outside of
bookstores) were excellent outlets for increasing sales. In many of
these, customers could find separate stands with best-selling, popular market evangelical books. Invariably the themes of these centered on personal problems and inspirational uplift. Also, older
publishing firms such as Harper and Row, Doubleday, and Scott,
Foresman added "evangelical" titles for the first time to their offerings; their previous works had been scholarly and mainline
Protestant. The catalogs and diversity of offerings (for all age
groups, price ranges and levels of sophistication) among the evangelical publishers by 1977 indicate they had become as competitive
and sophisticated as any secular firm.[8]

Not all observers were convinced all this was more than a
fad. One veteran editor, John Garvey, argued that the cult of celebrities in the born again camp presented a form of religious faith
which was domesticated -- "get it down to a cozy level, make God
a buddy." This was all too cute and familiar, "the promise of the
Bible gets whittled down to a success story" -- "some crooked pol
or fame-crazed celebrity gets saved and stops drinking and horsing
around -- that's what Jesus is for." Customers could find books on
Christian weight loss and Christian money management.[9]

To Garvey this was nothing new; church people had always
been "seduced" by the spirit of their age. What saddened him was
the interpretation that since such sales were so high, that proved
"America is becoming a religious nation." (This is not what I am
arguing in this chapter.) America was not going religious, but religion was becoming one more product, sold like everything else on
the market "where Jesus is reduced by making him fit our sense of

of life." Catering to mass taste is not by itself wrong, but "failing
to improve it is.... Christianity calls us (Phil. 4:8) to present the
true, the honorable, the just, the pure, the lively, the gracious,
the excellent, the worthy of praise...."[10]

Another evangelical publishing venture was the Christian
Yellow Pages, a business directory published in large cities across
the country; it appeared first in the mid-70s. Usually administered
by the offices of the National Association of Evangelicals, the directories contained advertisements from retailers "who are of 'like
faith', not expecting discount prices, but expecting honesty, quality, good service, and the satisfaction of helping another Christian." To be included, advertisers had to sign a statement saying
he or she was a born again Christian believer, and "accepts Jesus
Christ as...personal Lord and Savior and acknowledges Jesus as
the Son of God."[11] These have been revised annually, suggesting
they were being well received.

Some readers, however, were not pleased; sharp criticism came
from the National Council of Churches and other groups. The N.C.C.
called the Pages a "parody" of the advertising of the Second Jewish
Catalog (1976) which had a directory of goods and services "especially pertinent to Jewish life." There were no restrictions on the
advertisers there. The N.C.C. pointed out that the Christian Yellow
Pages became a threat to American communities, when ministers were
asked for answers on whether to "buy Christian." Prof. Marty suggests that such directories are "offensive to Jews and every other
kind of Gentile." The evangelicals reply that the Pages are not
against anyone, only for the evangelicals. Marty, in turn rejected
that, noting that litigation against the Pages was starting in some
courts.[12]

One final indication of new interest in evangelical publishing
emerged from the sharp increase in sales and improved quality of
the material of several non-denominational evangelical journals.
Magazines such as Christianity Today, Moody Monthly, Faith at
Work, Eternity, Christian Life and Christian Herald have all become more widely read than even five years ago. Given their wide

diversity of emphasis (some are more scholarly, others more popular or inspirational), all are also vehicles for advertising a wide
variety of religious goods, items not generally available in retail
outlets. The journals advertised tape cassettes, audio-visual equipment, label buttons, jewelry, bumper stickers, and similar items.

One casualty among them developed. An ambitious, bi-monthly
newspaper, National Courier, started publication in 1975 with the
policy of bringing "the mind of Christ to bear on the events of the
day." It failed within two years, the best explanation being that
with its heavy neo-Pentecostal accent, its readers were not that
much interested in the world around them. The stories were too
much alike; the market really did have a saturation point.[13] At the
same time, a less well organized but zesty evangelical underground press emerged during the 70s in journals such as Radix,
Sojourners, The Other Side and The Wittenburg Door. These generally were more critical, more socially sensitive and most invariably
managed to display a lively sense of humor.[14]

Without doubt, the 70's revival found it most far reaching
means of winning souls for Christ through television, "the electronic
church." Its influence in spreading revival into every part of the
nation was immense, so vast and pervasive as to be truly immea-
surable. Even today, the many born again programs continue to
grow rapidly in influence and strength. Revival, 70's style, had
found its best medium.

The roots of such strength reach back into the awakening of
the 1960s. Television, rather than radio or the newspapers, was
ideally suited to bring home to the public the full impact of the
events of those tumultuous years; the assasinations, the riots, the
war, and "the gargantuan, slow motion disaster of Watergate." The
most perceptive critic of this movement, Virginia Stem Owens, concludes "that real life (otherwise known as 'live action') was wed-
ded to movie-life with undreamed of repercussions in the American
consciousness. With a subtle ontological reversal, what was real
became what was televisable.... Real life exists in the shared tech-
nological sensory extensions of ourselves. Human activity is real
for us only insofar as it participates in those shared sensations."[15]

The electronic church preachers, both those starting off in the 60s and those rising to the top in the next decade, see television as one means to answer the call of the Great Commission, using "the most effective model for communication they know -- image advertising. Its success makes old-fashioned apologetics look like an archeological oddity. Catechisms are replaced by conferences on life-style." [16]

Religious television had begun when the medium itself came into popularity in the early 1950s. Among the first to utilize its potential were, of course, Billy Graham, then Oral Roberts, Herbert and Garner Ted Armstrong, Rex Humbard, and a little later, Robert Schuller. Several other free-lancers made their bids for national acceptance also, but by the early 70s those listed above were the only ones to grow financially and in general public acceptance. They used television primarily as the means of bringing well organized church or revival services into the nation's living rooms. They added some entertainment ingredients: national celebrities, skilled soloists, massed choruses. Yet a viewer could perceive that these programs were close to, if not identical with, regular services.

Then, in the mid-1970s, a breakthrough in format emerged quite spontaneously from the then little known 700 Club show of Pat Robertson. It would transform the electronic church into the primary means of winning souls for the 70's revival. During a 700 Club telethon a viewer called in with a pledge. Immediately the pledge-taker, visible for all to see, started to pray with the caller. Television quite unexpectedly had become a two-way responsive medium.[17] Robertson and his staff quickly expanded that format, turning the program into a nightly phone-in enterprise. To it they added many of the trappings of the secular late-night talk shows: the major star with an opening monologue, a co-host to feed the star straight lines, guest celebrities giving brief but fervent testimonials, guest singers or instrumentalists, choruses with men in three-piece suits and short hair and women in floor length gowns (often with more than a bit of decolletage) singing both old gospel hymns and contemporary songs of praise.

Robertson had set a model which others quickly duplicated and embroidered. A former announcer of his, Jim Bakker, broke with his employer to start the PTL network with an almost identical format. His autobiography Move That Mountain (1976) details his motives. After reaching stardom with the 700 Club (or, the Christian Broadcast Network) he stated that "the eighth day of November, 1972 arrived, and as I dressed for work, the Lord spoke to me, I want you to resign your job at CBN today." Not liking that order, Bakker asked instead that if the Lord would sell his house, Bakker would then resign. "No", the Lord answered, "you must resign first, and then I will sell your house." After several monts of soul searching, and consulting as a free-lance specialist to independent religious stations, Bakker directed a station in Los Angeles. Then he felt led to Charlotte, North Carolina, and from there the PTL program zoomed quickly to national prominence.[18]

Funding drives for both programs had been conducted by mail and during the programs themselves. Bakker's letter, commercially printed, looked like a personal letter to each potential giver. In it he underlined phrases such as "I'd like you to become my personal friend...become a PTL Partner.... For you are not alone in your troubles. I'll always be there when you need me. Make your commitment today..." for which the donor would receive "your very own copy of our New Partner Bible! I'm depending on you."[19]

The programs themselves make no effort to duplicate the kind of worship services of a Graham or Humbard. They instead present inspiration, information on upcoming mass rallies (such as the electronic churches sponsored in April, 1980 billed as "Jesus For Washington"), encouragement for viewers to phone the waiting counselors with personal problems, and Robertson's and Bakker's interpretations of current events, usually based on a very explicitly pre-millennial Second Coming foundation. Both these shows also welcome neo-Pentecostal expressions; a prophecy might break out, a

tongue may be spoken, a healing may occur -- all exciting fare for
the viewer.

No concrete means exist to measure how many souls were har-
vested by these programs. They simply do not keep those kinds of
statistics the way a Graham office tallies its nightly converts during a crusade. What can be pinpointed with some accuracy is the
financial support for these programs. The Wall Street Journal on
May 19 presented the 1978 figures. Graham's programs brought in
twenty eight million dollars a year by then; Oral Roberts programs
collected some sixty million dollars; before their collapse the
Armstrongs were taking in seventy five million annually. Humbard
had a variation for his fifty million plus programming: on 335 stations the services from his church had a technicolor cross 100 feet
high, made up of 4700 light bulbs in red, white or blue so that he
could flash the cross in 60 different light combinations. In Garden
Grove, California, Schuler, besides erecting a seventeen million dol-
lar glass cathedral, collects over ten million a year. Bakker
brought in over twenty five million annually and Robertson has
gifts of some thirty million a year. Unquestionably, these figures
were greater in 1979 but as yet, no reliable source of information
on them has been published.[20] The 700 Club and PTL are also on
cable television, reaching all sections of the nation with their own
stations plus buying airtime from the established outlets.[21]

As popular and influential as these programs are with many
viewers, they have attracted considerable scrutiny and criticism
by careful observers, even to a full discussion by specialists, supporters, and critics alike at a national conference in December,
1979, sponsored by the National Council of Churches.[22] The major
thrust of dissent comes from those who argue that, with the obvious exception of shut-ins, religious television becomes a substitute
for participating in the community church, and draws money from
that institution. It makes "feeling religious" or profound worship
too simple, with armchairs and coffee available at the "service".
It draws too often on the secular world for its tone, its format
and its standards of success.

Specifically, observers argue, since church membership demands discipleship (and many evangelicals demonstrate that), some
kind of sacrifice, some dedication is best nourished by live preaching and the sacraments, by one's social involvement in the local
worshipping community. The television viewer, however, is cut off
from all of that. Marty suggests one reason for the decline in
church membership and attendance in recent years is that people
now can stay at home to watch the latest full color spectacular,
"ruffle-shirted, pink-tuxedoed men and the high-coiffeured, low neck-
lined celebrity women who talk about themselves under the guise
of Born Again autobiographies." Sunday morning services have
"Holy Ghost entertainers caress microphones among supporting foun-
tains and a high professional charismatic leader entertains them."
Why, then, he asks, should people get dressed up, go out to hear
the off-key choirs, and ordinary preachers who lack well prepared
appeals for funds? Another critic finds that some who contribute to
the TV programs would not contribute to a local congregation.[23]

The comfort of watching television at home rather than worshipping at church bothers other observers. They see the danger
that the electronic church threatens the most vital institution to
the organized denominations -- the local congregation. What the local parish can offer is people working together in a common mission, supporting and growing with each other. Since the church as
an institution is under attack in our day, its support must not be
allowed to slip away any further. Finally, critics worry that so
many of the programs preach old-time hell fire and damnation,
talk freely about the End Times and the world coming apart, yet
át the same time they present "an image of success -- a thriving,
expanding institution using with skill society's most influential
medium."[24]

Evangelical leaders note the several dangers involved in electronic evangelism. Some ads for religious programs are little more
than promotions for the record albums or the books of the born
again celebrity guests. Viewers are encouraged to watch so they

may "feel better", not to understand what it means to take up one's Cross and follow Christ.

An extensive criticism has come from Virginia Stem Owens, who summarizes a penetrating analysis with these words:

> It really is a very simple and obvious proposition I make: a person, whether human or divine, cannot be known -- as a person rather than an image -- except by immediate presence. If we want to project an image, either of Christians or the church, we can do that by means of television, magazines, books, billboards, movies, bumper stickers, buttons, records, and posters. If we want people to know Christ, we must be there face to face, bearing Christ within us. And therein lies the great danger. A rejection of Christ becomes a rejection of ourselves, individually and painfully. Perhaps this is why we do not want to take the risk and why we are so eager to pile up a barricade of media technology be-ween us and the unpredictable outside world.[25]

Another evangelical source, Eternity magazine in its May, 1978, issue presented another far reaching evaluation. Acknowledging the advantages of being able to witness more freely in more places nowadays than ever before (including television), the authors suggest some caution is in order. First, there is the exploitation of the newly born again entertainers (e.g., Carol Lawrence) who need religious nurturing more than a filled-up itinerary. Second, Christian show business can become excessive and extravagant. The plush interiors of Christian supper clubs and settings for television programs can create a clubby, elitist atmosphere for Christian "beautiful people". Third, this business can "go Hollywood"; by the utilization of razzmatazz techniques already used by secular television, Christians are being conditioned to expect the same atmosphere on their programs -- and some electronic church programs give them that. Fourth, there always remains the danger of competition among the leaders of the top programs. Christians often do not work well together; each has his or her own empire and wants to keep it under control. Hence, show business becomes bogged down in personalities, rather than institutions, such as the organized church. Finally, as in every situation in life, one needs to remember the need for "tremendous humility before God."[26]

As penetrating as the criticisms are, the electronic church continued through the 70s to present the born again option, offer counsel to the perplexed, instruct viewers in its understanding of the Christian faith and, above all, to harvest souls. Its aggressive sell methods usually repelled not only non-evangelicals, but many of those within the pressers on camp. Yet the latter in one sense were responsible for the enthusiasm for this form of popular religion. Remaining fixed in their scholarly corners, refusing to get into the mass market, they created a vacuum which the electronic church quickly filled.

The popularity of electronic evangelism helped strengthen another distinctive feature of the late 70s revival -- the popularity of famous personalities in high places freely testifying to their born again experience. Surely it was no coincidence that "The Year of the Evangelical," 1976, was also the nation's first sustained exposure to candidate Jimmy Carter and to Watergate's chief hatchetman, Charles Colson, author of Born Again. This facet soon became a virtual growth industry, capped perhaps by the publication of a book Top Entertainers are Born Again; in it the testimonials of Johnny Cash, Pat Boone, Anita Bryant, Carol Lawrence and the Colonel of Kentucky Fried Chicken, among others were given.[27]

No way exists to prove how in any direct manner these personalities actually helped seekers to find the born again experience. What can be said is that this phenomenon helped give greater legitimacy to instant conversion Christianity than had existed before in revivalist history.

The born again were no longer considered simply fanatics or wishful thinkers or holy rollers; now even the President of the United States was one of the chosen. That was a boost, or better, one more ingredient in the unique constellation which made the late 1970's revival what it was compared to earlier movements. Further, the presence of celebrities gave born againism more publicity than it might well have received otherwise.

In sum for Part Three, the evidence given there about the Gothards, Morgans, Christian schools and related enterprises as well as electronic evangelism, touched millions of lives, offered attractive role models and helped legitimize revivalism to an extent unparalleled in American history. Yet, as suggested earlier, each revival has its own personality. This one was no different because, just when many observers believed it would run its natural course, the late 70's revival turned into a volatile, explosive political crusade. Or at least one substantial wing of the new egangelicalism joined the lists for combat at the ballot boxes. The entrance of evangelicals (and fundamentalists) into national elective politics perhaps should not have surprised Americans because the new cause was both a fitting conclusion to many of the trends which had shaped the popular revival, and at the same time, was a clear harbinger of new things to come. The political dimension of the late 70's revival, as will be argued in Part Four, suggests evangelicalism for all its fragmentation, its inner divisiveness, its several forms of superficiality, had reached a level of cultural maturation new to its history. Having two successive born again Christians in the White House stood as a fitting symbol to the new power and sophistication of the evangelicals. They saw revival as politics, politics as revival. Such a transformation requires our closest attention.

PART FOUR

EVANGELICALS IN THE WHITE HOUSE

CHAPTER XIII

THE FIRST EVANGELICAL IN THE WHITE HOUSE

INTRODUCTION

One of the most fascinating elements in a religious revival is that the decision to be born again, to answer the altar call, leads the converts into many, widely varying forms of expressing what the new life now entails. In the 19th century slave traders who came forward became abolitionist preachers; baseball players became showman evangelists. In our century instant conversion has led to physical and emotional healing, to forsaking posh life-styles, to working among the poor, to reclaiming the land and its resources -- the list goes on.

The late 70's revival concentrated in its early expression on major theological and ethical issues, as well as personal uplift and inspiration. Then, suddenly, it took on the personality of a political crusade. In itself this was not a totally new phenomenon in American history. William Jennings Bryan in 1896, a born again Christian if ever one existed, used politics as revival, reform as crusade. So too devout Woodrow Wilson in 1916 sought to convince Americans their role as mediator to end World War I was a crusade worthy of the greatest sacrifice. Barry Goldwater in 1964 attempted to convince Americans that the great moral issues could be resolved, or at least mediated, by good people, committed to the tenets of evangelical Christianity.[1]

Yet the leaders of the 1970's revival wanted both revival (instant conversion), and moral crusade fused together in one unified contest. That was the unique quality of the evangelicals' decision to forsake their disdain of the political arena and turn to it, master it, and make it work for them. Theirs was another way in which the born again respond to the impact of knowing they have been saved. This time being 'saved' meant quite a bit more than it did to those who had walked up the sawdust trails over the decades. Being 'saved' in the 1980 parlance meant (1) accepting Christ as one's Lord and Savior -- that was familiar enough, but it also meant (2) taking secular political power and using it for moral crusading to save by revival the nation from total collapse. Revival became politics, politics was the road to revival. Salvation was available not only at the altar but at the ballot box. Revival, indeed, works its own unpredictable ways in the lives of the born again.

JIMMY CARTER

The emergence of Jimmy Carter during the takeoff years of the mid-1970's revival gave that resurgence a credibility and a hope no earlier revival had known. Evangelicals hailed his election as proof that they had not only been accepted by mainstream America, but also that evangelical faith was well on its way to dominating the religious scene. It had one of its kind in the Oval Office; it had access to the most powerful leader of the world. It could ask for nothing larger.

Carter himself expressed a school of born again Christianity which was instantly recognizable by all evangelicals, but not necessarily representative of the center of that movement. He was fond of quoting Soren Kierkegaard's aphorism that "every man is an exception," here meaning every evangelical is his own person, not a stereotype of undistinguishable believer. He stood with all evangelicals in talking about his conversion experience; he continued teaching Bible studies on Sunday mornings before, during, and after his Presidency using the scriptures alone as self-explanatory for the day's topic. He tried to instill in his Presidency a sense of warmth, trust and fidelity to the traditional values of family he had known throughout his life. Eschewing older evangelical taboos against dancing, alcohol, movies, and working on Sunday, he created the image of a born againer being freed from pietism, yet eager to share his foundational faith. His was an embodiment of a newer, more sophisticated and pluralistic evangelicalism than that of an earlier day.[2]

Yet it was not representative of the center of the born again position. Carter sought to lead, to persuade, to inspire by personal example rather than by using propositional doctrine as his final authority. The formal theology and doctrine he knew was kept well in the background when he made his witness. His would be more the pressing on than the holding fast commitment. Bill Moyers asked once, "What drives you?" Carter replied

> I don't know...exactly how to express it.... I feel I have one life to live. I feel like that God wants me to do the best I can with it. And that's quite often my major prayer. Let me live my life so that it will be meaningful. When I have a sense of peace and self assurance...that what I'm doing is the right thing, I assume maybe in an unwarranted way, that that's doing God's will.[3]

The career of Jimmy Carter is so well known as to need no review here. What can be considered is how his evangelical convictions led him to the kind of public leadership he exhibited until he left the Oval Office in 1981. As pressers on before him had learned, Carter discovered in working up through Georgia politics to the governorship that the conversion experience and earnest witnessing were no guarantees that their believers would be better leaders. The rules by which one was elected to office allowed for little of the soft-spoken pressing on in which Carter believed.

To be specific, the candidate seeking office in the American system would first have to point out why the incumbent or rival

rival candidate had a less satisfactory program than his own; a sense of dissatisfaction with the status quo among voters had to be created. The voter had to be led to believe better programs were possible. Once the discontent was established and hope for the future offered, the candidate had to convince the voters that his program would work, that the answers rested with casting one's vote for "the man who". A sense of high expectation, of hope for a better program was indispensible for victory.

Yet as office seekers everywhere have learned, this was a risky course. It enhanced the voters' awareness of what was wrong with present policies, risking the chance of creating cynicism or indifference. Equally risky was the raising of hopes for improvement to such a high plane that genuine improvement could never be achieved, leading again in a cyclical form to disenchantment and cynicism.

Carter obviously was aware in 1976 of these risks, but chose to make the run for the White House. He was willing to stake the success of the programs he would offer by asking the voters to judge how well he had answered two questions: "Can our government be honest, decent, open, fair, and compassionate? Can our government be competent?"[4]

He knew the enormous spread of cynicism, mistrust and indifference towards the national government following the debacles of Watergate and Vietnam. He knew also his fellow Democratic rivals for the Presidency enjoyed national stature. Carter chose to run as an outsider, freed from the influence of Washington and full of new and achievable goals so that America could enjoy, as his campaign autobiography title asked, Why Not the Best? After surviving, with some losses, the long obstacle course of primaries, he was elected President. He was assisted both by his outsider image and because voters continued to blame the Republican nominee, Gerald Ford, for issuing an unconditional pardon to Richard Nixon. The first authentic born again evangelical moved into the White House in January, 1977.

The balance of this chapter avoids a chronological narrative of Carter's term. Longer and more detailed accounts of it are readily available. What will be attempted here is an overview of the major developments grouped together in topical units, although obviously they intertwined and stretched out over the full four years. The thesis I put forward is that on balance Carter's record failed more frequently on the crucial issues than it succeeded, and that this outcome suggests something of the fortunes during the late 1970s of revivalism as popular religion. Put in other terms, the Carter administration suggests the accuracy of Reinhold Niebuhr's argument that "moral man" does not necessarily have superior resources to reform "immoral society". A turning, a born again conversion may well put an individual in a more rewarding position to receive forgiveness and grace; that experience, however, as the Carter record shows, failed to be translated successfully into the larger public setting.

The suggestion has been made above that Carter was a moral man. The public opinion polls consistently throughout 1977-80 indicated the voters continued to give him very high marks on integrity, trustworthiness, and honesty regardless of what they thought about his specific policies. Carter, however, ran into considerable difficulty from the very beginning of his days in the Oval Office because he could not convince many of the voters that at least two of his closest friends, Bert Lance and brother Billy Carter were equally moral. Lance's financial maneuverings and Billy's relations with the government of Libya sounded all too much to the general public as friends using the White House for personal advantage.

In foreign policy, Carter early on made a bold initiative for human rights. He told Soviet dissident Andrei Sakharov, "The American people and our government will continue our firm commitment to promote respect for human rights not only in our country but also abroad. We shall use our good offices to seek the release of prisoners of conscience and . . . to shape a world responsive to human aspirations in which nations of differing cultures and histories can live side by side in peace and justice." He believed it was right to criticize the repression of basic personal freedoms in other countries even when this meant attacking the internal policies of those nations under American scrutiny. But faced at the same time with evidence of increasing Soviet imperialism, Carter backed away from criticizing human rights violations in nations such as South Korea where the government worked closely with the United States to keep the U.S.S.R. at bay.

Carter spent considerable energy in resisting the pressures of those Americans who wanted to increase governmental spending for new weaponry. He vetoed a bill to develop the B-1 bomber, he halted production of neutron bombs, he put his reputation on the line to obtain a SALT II mutual disarmament treaty with the Soviets. Yet he lacked the political adroitness to convince key Senate leaders and the American public that his was the better course. As a result, defense spending increased, SALT II was shelved, and production of highly expensive weaponry continued.

Major victories were won with the turning over of the Panama Canal to the Republic of Panama and with the highly emotional reconciliation of Egypt and Israel at the 1978 Camp David accord. The latter achievement raised his reputation around the world to the level of a true peacemaker. However, he (nor perhaps anyone) could not prevent the Israeli government in ensuing months from continuing to refuse the inclusion of the Palestinian Liberation Organization in any permanent boundary settlements in Israel.

Late in the administration further setbacks occurred when Carter allowed the deposed Shah of Iran to leave his exile for medical treatment in the United States, leading to the capture of 52 hostages in Teheran. An aborted military rescue of them failed and despite considerable internal turmoil among competing Iranian political factions, Carter could not find a formula for release of the captives until his last week in office. So too when the Soviets invaded Afghanistan, Carter responded with the boycott of the Olympic games in Moscow, summer 1980, resumption of the registration for the draft, and the Carter Doctrine which told the Soviets in essence America would resist with military means any territorial expansion of the Russians into the oil-rich Persian Gulf nations. Those two flashpoints, Iran and Afghanistan, touched off something the President had not intended but could not have helped know might occur -- a volatile wave of jingoism spreading across the country, resorting to war if necessary to force the Iranians and Soviets to comply fully with American demands.

In domestic matters, Carter met similarly disastrous situations. Not being able to force the OPEC nations to stop the huge price increases in petroleum, he and the nation watched the impact on what soon became galloping inflation, running near twenty per cent in 1980. A variety of programs for relief, rearrangement of interest rates and jawboning failed to hold down inflation. So, too, after some early success in lowering the unemployment rates, the President watched as that also started an upward spiral, reaching disastrous levels for major American automobile manufacturers by the summer of 1980.

It was here that the weakness of the American political system revealed itself so vividly. To be elected Carter had to convince the voters his programs would succeed. When they didn't, through a combination of both forces beyond his control and policies of his design, he was trapped.

In other domestic matters, he sent to Congress far reaching reform programs for welfare, conservation, urban renewal, and tax reform. For a variety of reasons including his failure to establish a harmonious working relationship with the lawmakers, these programs were either stalled or came out in far different form than he had proposed.

In none of these cases (save those perhaps of Lance and Billy Carter) was there any hint of imperial presidency or wrongdoing on Carter's part. Like the academic pressers on, Carter's impressive intentions, vast good will and honorable motives quickly reached an impasse on virtually every major domestic and foreign issue. During the summer of 1979, Carter recognized the general drift, sought to locate its cause, and reverse its momentum. After spending several days at Camp David with both close advisers and with representatives of many areas of national life, he delivered a "Sunday Night Sermon" to the nation. He argued that America was continuing to experience the loss of faith started earlier in the decade. Americans, he said, were preoccupied with individual goals rather than the national interest. "Too many of us now worship self-indulgence and consumption." Too many Americans identified themselves by what they owned, not by what they contributed to society. Americans would have to lower their expectations of material reward, unlimited use of energy, and an ever-rising standard of living. America, in short, could not solve its problems by ignoring them, by continuing to indulge in materialistic consumption without paying the prices of inflation, unemployment and continuing decline of respect by the rest of the world. As one editorialist responded to the sermon, "Carter was not blaming and he was not accusing; he was identifying the problems as belonging to the realm of the mysterious, the human conflict between wanting everything and realizing that limits were required."[5]

That speech made little impact on his declining popularity in the polls. It did, however, offer the rival Republican Party the ammunition it needed to take its turn (in the July, 1980 convention) to locate the cause of the national malaise directly in the policies of Carter. To overcome the pessimism they said the President was preaching in his 'sermon', they called on Americans to believe, as former President Ford stated, "There is no problem Americans can't solve if they put their minds to it." The cycle of criticism, promise, defeat, deflation and cynicism had started over.

Would it have made any measurable difference had Carter not been a born again evangelical? We have no way of knowing. What we can conclude is that despite its failures, Carter did attempt a moral presidency, in contrast to the amoral pragmatism of other nations. One supporter of his concluded that the President "has done exactly what we called on him to do in establishing a moral presidency and . . . will be saddened if it turns out that such a presidency is not viable. . . ."[6]

Carter was not rejected because he was an evangelical. He had, if nothing else, convinced the born again that one of them could hold the highest office in the land. Only his kind of evangelicalism was not in the mainstream of that religious tradition. The many frustrations and the failures during his administration served, with other forces, to reinvigorate the holders fast evangelicals. That most of them were also Republicans helped make that union more speedily. The holders fast, divided and disjointed as they were in academia, were moving in a much different direction in the world of elective politics. They watched as Carter slipped, floundered and failed. At the time that was happening, they were gearing up their machinery, girding their loins, to put holding fast evangelicals in the highest offices in the land. And, as we will see in the next two chapters, they did just that.

CHAPTER XIV

THE TRANSFORMATION OF
EVANGELICAL POLITICAL INVOLVEMENT

While the popular and scholarly forms of the late 1970s revival unfolded over the country, few participants knew that the energy and enthusiasm created for born again faith was being studied and harnessed into direct political expression. This new dimension was not secretive; the preachings of the television pulpiteers such as Robertson and Falwell were public as were the activities of those professional vote and fund raisers seeking to bring born again candidates to the voters for the 1980 campaign. But few observers saw the potential connections among all these strands. The intertwining of those connections, however, as we will explore now, marked the cultural maturation of evangelicalism in America.

Born again revivalism was flourishing not only because of the assurances it brought believers about their eternal destiny but because it seemed a divinely inspired backlash or criticism against the believers' perceived decline of morality in America. As a movement, revivalism had a common enemy -- immorality (sometimes referred to as "secular humanism" see pp. 110-13). That common enemy had several ingredients, the total of which seemed so powerful as to be almost irreversible in American life. They included the practice of legal abortion following the Supreme Court decision of 1973, the continuing ban on religious exercises in public schools, the demands by the women's movement for equal rights, the greater accessibility to materials many people considered pornographic, the greater militancy of homosexuals -- the list could be extended at some length.

To many born again, encouraged by the electronic preachers to accept this diagnosis, these were satanic symptoms that America was collapsing. Obviously these events didn't just happen; specific, identifiable causes for them could be located if the effort were made. The most obvious source was the political party in power -- the Democrats with their majorities in Congress and their domestic liberal policies in effect across the nation.

Political observers noticed that slowly after 1972 an increasing number of evangelicals and fundamentalists perceived that the Democratic party in 1972 had "embarked on an ideological journey to the left." Senator George McGovern was seen as the front for those who wanted to encourage the 'moral revolution' in this country to grow; more rights for women, no restrictions on gays, abortion on demand; in short, this analysis went, the Democrats were now "a leftist coalition."[1]

Yet evangelicals were not yet quite ready to admit that active national politicing could reverse the downward spiral. They knew Carter was one of them and could well reach the White House. Why not wait until he had an opportunity to serve? Unknown in most born again circles, however, was the presence of a small but highly efficient group of religiously and politically conservative fund and vote raisers -- the direct mail organizers. They were not ready to wait to see what Carter would do; they wanted to move now and in their judgment the only way the moral decline of the nation could be reversed would be to have highly moral men elected to the highest positions in the government.[2]

The structure for such work was already in place. As early as 1968 Richard Vigurie, once executive director of Young Americans for Freedom, had become a finance adviser to George Wallace, running that year for the Presidency. Vigurie had collected several thousand names of conservative donors. Over the next years he added thousands more, finding the special, often single issues the

voter/donor was interested in seeing enacted. In the mid-1970s he
was joined by Paul Weyrich who headed up an issues lobby, Committee for the Survival of a Free Congress, and Howard Phillips,
leader of a grassroots organizing group, Conservative Caucus. Together they offered their services to conservative congressmen: com-
puterized mailing lists of donors, specific issues on which conservatives could run and win, and ways and means to organize successfully on the local level.[3]

The trio, who formed a loose coalition, found a growing demand for their services from Senators such as Jessie Helms and
Strom Thurmond. They also found an increasing number of voters
expressing concern over the trends in public morality which the
direct mail solicitors were bringing to their attention. From this
emerged an even larger, umbrella organization known as the National Conservative Political Action Committee (NCPAC). That was a co-
ordinating group headed by Terry Dolan to keep track of what issues interested the voters, what appeals brought in funds, which
candidates for Congress seemed vulnerable, and what special interest blocs of voters seemed ready to move in the conservatives' direction.

As more funds came in, more sophisticated means of plumbing
public opinion developed, and skill in using direct mail by computers increased, this group of holders fast was finding itself
able to win increasing respect from other conservatives in and outside the evangelical and fundamentalist churches. As the leaders
realized the trend towards single issues among voters was continuing to grow, they decided to break with precedent and organize
the faithful believers into an action-oriented political voter bloc.
Neither Vigurie, Phillips or Weyrich was well known enough to
give any proposed national organization the visibility it needed.
After careful screening and interviewing, in June, 1979, they made
their choices: Jerry Falwell, pastor of Thomas Road Baptist Church,
Lynchburg, Virginia and national celebrity television preacher.
Supporting the choice of Falwell to head the evangelical, fundamentalist bloc was the Rev. Robert Billings, head of a newly created

lobby, National Christian Action Coalition and later to be appointed by Gov. Reagan as chief liason between his team and the religious voter blocs.

After considerable planning the direct mailers and Falwell, with his staff, announced the formation of the "Moral Majority." This would be a political action program to bring the issues to the voters, get the shirking ones registered, raise funds, tell the voters who would be qualified among office seekers to stop the moral decay in the country and, in sum, hold fast. They sensed the strong tide running in favor of evangelicalism in the nation; now was the time to direct some of that power into political channels.[4]

Their actions blended nicely with the mainstream of evangelicalism, contrasted to that of Carter, which put its priorities on doctrine, authority, judgment, taking the issue to the enemy by direct action rather than by personal example. Moral Majority was soon joined by another similar group, out of Pasadena, California, named "Christian Voice." More explicitly than Falwell's organization, Christian Voice called for the election of specific candidates, its chief hope being Gov. Reagan. It also introduced two familiar political campaign instruments into the upcoming campaign, the "report card" and "target lists" of office seekers to defeat. Both were of longstanding use in American history. What was unusual about their use by Christian Voice, Moral Majority and National Christian Action Coalition was the holding fast foundations of their positions.

Each group issued report cards, lists of specific bills or appointments facing specific congressmen. The holders fast explained that each of these was a moral issue; a vote one way would promote morality in America, a vote the other way would indicate the lawmaker was immoral or at least not fully attuned to the moral dimensions of the issues being discussed. Each Senator and Representative was rated by the action groups as to how moral his or her vote was according to a checklist of items they had determined would indicate the depth of morality of the lawmaker. These included matters such as ERA, federal funding of abortion, gay

rights, school busing, religious exercises in public schools -- the
whole gamut of issues which had been building up since the late
1960s among the conservative voters of America. [5]

Throughout early 1980 and well into the summer, the direct
mailers sent what Richard Vigurie later estimated to be close to
one billion pieces of literature on these issues to voters. There
those who the mailers understood would be motivated by this kind
of appeal could see just what was wrong with America: it had immoral leaders directing its destiny. What should they do about
them? The mailers, plus electronic preachers, such as Falwell and
James Robinson of Fort Worth, presented the second instrument for
political campaigning, the target list (or as the jargon of the day
had it, the 'hit' list) of Senators and Representatives up for election to be defeated. It was in essence blending revival and politics; stating the way to revive morality and God's blessing on this
land again was to organize the voters, get them to understand the
moral issues involved, encourage them to share their money, show
them how to evangelize against the targeted lawmakers among their
friends, and hence, revive America.

The leaders such as Vigurie, Dolan and others were politically pragmatic enough to realize they could not defeat every Senator or Representative seeking re-election who had not shown what
the report cards deemed to be enough morality. So after careful
research, the mailers and preachers selected six United States Senators, all liberal Democrats, for special attention: Birch Bayh of
Indiana, Gaylord Nelson of Wisconsin, John Culver of Iowa, George
McGovern of South Dakota, Alan Cranston of California and Frank
Church of Idaho. They also selected some 35 members of the House
of Representatives for defeat. Much of the ever increasing treasury
of funds garnered by the direct mail techniques went into these
states. In most cases the candidates running against the incum-
bents welcomed the money and the support of Moral Majority and
Christian Voice. [6]

In the summer of 1980 all of this suddenly captured the front
pages of the newspapers and the lead stories on the television and

radio newscasts. This was indeed something very new in American religious and political life. The media and the general public well understood traditional religious revival, but this political dimension was new, baffling and to some frightening. Never before had evangelicals or fundamentalists entered directly into the political world; never before had their absolutist positions drawn frcm their holding-fast, inerrancy positions been brought into campaigning. This kind of revival was something new and to those opposed to it, unpredictable and thus impossible to know how to block.

Thus the revival of the late 70s, as every major one earlier in American history, took its own distinctive turn. Its scholars were feuding, its popularizers were profiting, and now its politicians were calling for a whole new way to express one's born again convictions. To some observers, this three-headed movement looked like no movement at all; to others it seemed to suggest that perhaps the evangelicals were becoming the mainstreamers.[7] It might all end quickly; it might well be a media event. Only the test of taking revival as politics to the people could tell whether those impressions were sound. As it would turn out, the holders fast would prevail. It was they, not the liberals or mainliners, who mastered the new technology of computers and television and turned them to their advantage. It was the holders fast who learned how to read public opinion and present to the voter/donor the kind of information the latter wanted to hear or read. It was the New Right who studied past political campaigning techniques and took the best of them for their own. In brief, the holders fast chose the last years of the 1970s to move directly and totally into politics, breaking with their past. That is another way of saying they had reached cultural maturation. The Carter's pressers on were left outside.

CHAPTER XV

THE CAMPAIGN OF 1980:
ANOTHER EVANGELICAL IN THE WHITE HOUSE

The continuing strength of the evangelical resurgence of the 1970s carried in it enough strength to bring one kind of evangelical into the White House who replaced another kind, both of whom were challenged by the strongest of the outsider candidates for the same office, himself a well known evangelical. This trio of candidates, all born again, all witnessing evangelicals -- Ronald Reagan, Jimmy Carter and John Anderson -- simply an astounding indication of evangelical maturation. What can be said at the very least is that for none of them, did their born again faith hurt their election chances. At the most we can conclude the temper of the voters in November, 1980, wanted the kind of certainty and authority that evangelicals exuded. Only by that date, a different kind of evangelical was living in the White House. In this chapter we want to look at Reagan's kind of evangelical faith, his strategy and tactics, the clout that evangelical politics carried in America by that time, and conclude with a summation of politics as revival and of the late 70's revival itself.

Since his conversion away from politically liberal convictions in the 1950s, Ronald Reagan had moved slowly but visibly towards accepting a holding fast kind of evangelicalism. Himself a member of the Disciples of Christ denomination, he as a public figure (for example, Governor of California) avoided any overt show of sectarian loyalty while at the same time explaining his faith. He made known during the 1976 race for the Presidency where he stood.

Even before Falwell, the Moral Majority and the report cards, Governor Reagan in the Bicentennial year deplored the "wave of humanism and hedonism in the land. I think there is a hunger in this land for a spiritual revival, a return to a belief in moral absolutes -- the same morals upon which the nation was founded. When you go out across the country and meet the people you can't help but pray and remind God of II Chronicles 7:14 because the people of this country are not beyond redemption."

Right to the point he said, "I certainly know what the meaning of 'born again' is today among those who believe in that. I can't remember a time in my life when I didn't call on God.... In my own experience there came a time when there developed a new relationship with God and it grew out of need. So, yes, I have had an experience that could be described as 'born again'."[1]

Picking up on some of the themes the New Right developed into major campaign issues in 1980, Reagan in 1976 came out against any legislation legalizing homosexual acts between consenting adults. "I have always believed that the body of man-made laws must be founded upon the higher natural law. You can make immorality legal, but you cannot make it moral." On another 1980 theme, abortion, Reagan stated "I think it comes down to one simple answer: You cannot interrupt a pregnancy without taking a human life. And the only way we can justify taking a life in our Judeo-Christian tradition is in self-defense."[2]

Although he lost the Republican nomination for the Presidency that year to incumbent Gerald Ford, Reagan continued to carry his message and candidacy to the public. He made the usual vague statements shortly after the 1976 election about not knowing whether he would run again for the Presidency. All the while he was picking up holding fast support from evangelicals and fundamentalists who grew (as we saw earlier) increasingly disenchanted with the pressing on born againer, Jimmy Carter. Without explicitly endorsing him, the direct mail soliciters increased their mailings and their income when they concentrated through their constituents on the specific issues and general ideology of Reagan. When the

time came, finally, for candidates to declare themselves as choos-
ing to run for the primaries, Reagan made his plans clear -- an
all-out run for the Presidency.

Starting somewhere in early 1979 when his candidacy became
a sure thing, the holders fast and the professional vote/fund
raisers stepped up their programs to make 1980 the year for putting an authentic conservative in the White House. The several ingredients representative of the new evangelical/revival interest in
politics started to fall into a more predictable pattern. To the
Falwells, the Viguries, and the holders fast the candidacy of
Reagan would make worthwhile their best efforts to break with
past tradition and move directly into the political arena.[3]

Reagan moved cautiously but without a step backwards to
win over the evangelical vote. He knew the loyalty many of them
had towards Carter, the first authentic born againer in the White
House, and he could not, dared not call for Carter's defeat on the
basis of the Georgian's religious commitment, or lack of it. What
apparently came to be Reagan's strategy towards the evangelicals
through the 1980 primaries was to continue to make statements
about moral issues, to talk about a return to moral absolutes, to
state he would welcome the vote and support of any loyal American.
In that manner he would be interpreted by those evangelicals disenchanted with the President as saying he was with them but as
a candidate for the Presidency, he had to speak to the entire populace, not only evangelicals.[4]

Yet he also had to avoid sounding like a "me too" evangelical of the Carter persuasion. If he did, especially after John
Anderson entered the race, he would seem to be appealing to the
same voter sentiment as his two rivals, both with long track records as active in evangelical activities. Reagan apparently decided to remain above criticizing Carter's or Anderson's convictions,
while disagreeing with them on specific issues and at the same
time keeping up the talk about a return to absolutes. This he carried out with great success in the primaries from New Hampshire
in March to California in June.

Then came the magic moment, the nominating convention in Detroit during July. By that time all of his rivals had conceded defeat and the convention could be used as a coronation of the new candidate and the celebration of the new unity Republicans were praising as signs that the Grand Old Party was indeed the united new party for the future. Once nominated, Reagan seemingly made a mistake in New Right opinion by selecting George Bush for his running mate. Jerry Falwell had been in Reagan's hotel suite at Detroit trying to get the Governor to nominate a more conservative candidate. James Robinson later told his audiences he too was displeased with the nomination of Bush, but it was too late to change that now. [5]

Once nominated, Reagan brought out the next step in his strategy to win the evangelical vote; his approach was aimed without qualification at the holders fast. He chose as his liason officer with the religious blocs the Rev. Robert Billings, head of the National Christian Action Coalition, then a high official of Moral Majority. Billings personally was an extremely conservative spokeman for both political and religious issues -- a far step away from the more irenic pressing on position of Carter.[6] As Moral Majority and Christian Voice came under strong media criticism for their outspoken moralism, Reagan responded, "I'm going to be open to these people. In other words, I'm not going to separate myself from the people who elected us and sent us here." George Bush picked up on the theme by telling the press, "a lot of the views of the so-called Moral Majority are not extreme views."[7] Reagan was joining with the holders fast.

That strategy came close to falling apart at the moment of his direct identification with the hard liners. He, as well as Carter and Anderson, had been invited to address a gathering of Protestant ministers in Dallas in August; there the delegates would consider the issues, attend seminars on political organization and fund raising and generally get their motors tuned for the political campaign. Anderson and Carter declined the invitations but Reagan accepted. He chose the moment to make explicitly clear what he had in mind. Knowing to whom he was speaking he said, "I know you can't endorse me, but I want you to know that I endorse you and what you are doing."[8] As one sympathetic journalist noted, the delegates "were exuberant in their enchantment." They had in mind "nothing less than the launching of a Protestant crusade aimed at redeeming America, its morals and politics."[9]

Yet at that same conference disaster almost struck for the Reagan strategy. The current President of the Southern Baptist Convention, the Rev. Bailey Smith addressed the delegates: "It is interesting at great political rallies how you have a Protestant to pray and a Catholic to pray, and then you have a Jew to pray. With all due respect to these dear people, my friends, God Almighty does not hear the prayer of a Jew."[10]

That teaching was a familiar ingredient in fundamentalist theology. But it was made at the same time the representative of one of the two major parties was at the same meeting; the press wondered whether Reagan endorsed Bailey's statement. The New Right leaders understood the gravity of the situation, but their initial fence mending did little good. Robison rephrased Smith's remarks for those who objected to them by saying, "If a Jew trusts in Christ, then of course God hears that prayer." Falwell, by now a national celebrity, made his restatement, "God hears the prayers of every redeemed gentile and Jew." One reporter noted that Falwell was saying that "only those redeemed by Jesus Christ could have prayers answered." Falwell pleaded with the media that he was not anti-Semitic.[11]

Reagan heard the public outcry of disapproval of Smith, Robison and Falwell. He had "endorsed" the meeting and now it seemed he might be endorsing the hardline fundamentalist position on Jews being out of God's hearing range. The Governor moved quickly to repair the damage. On October 3, in Falwell's hometown he made a major campaign speech. In it he talked carefully about "Judeo-Christian values." Later at a press conference he was asked if he shared the views on Jews and prayers of the fundamentalists. "No," he replied, "since both the Christian and Judaic religions are based on the same God, the God of Moses. I'm quite sure that these prayers are heard. But then, I guess everyone can make his own interpretation of the Bible, and many individuals have been making different interpretations for a long time."[12]

That last sentence kept the controversy alive. Reagan had seemed to break with the holders fast until he suggested, as President Carter later noted, that Reagan was saying whether God heard the prayers of Jews was something on which reasonable men could disagree.[13] Finally, as receipts for Moral Majority started to drop as the criticisms of the issue grew, Falwell changed his mind. After consulting with Rabbi Marc Tannenbaum of the American Jewish Committee, Falwell stated, "This is a time for Catholics, Protestants, Jews, Mormons, and all Americans to rise above every effort to polarize us in our efforts to return this nation to a commitment to the moral principles on which America was built. America is a pluralistic republic. We cannot survive if we allow it to become anything less. God hears the cry of any sincere person who calls on Him"[14]

That statement, a clear reversal from his original position, put Falwell back in a more commanding position to lead the holders fast for Reagan and against the targeted Congressmen. As the results flowed in on Election Night, it became clear Reagan/Bush would take the top spot and that the Republican party would dominate the Senate while narrowing the Democratic lead in the House of Representatives. Five of the six targeted Senators (Cranston being the exception) lost to their challengers, a victory for which the New Right including the hardliners took credit.[15]

Obviously no foolproof method exists to prove precisely how effective holding fast support for Reagan helped him and the challengers to the targeted Senators win. What can be concluded with full confidence is that holding fast endorsement caused none of its recipients to lose. The television preachers and the direct mail soliciters, further, had outplanned, outworked, outspent and outmaneuvered their opposition. Evangelicals had helped put, first Carter in the White House, then finding him lacking, moved quickly

towards another variety of the born again. Whether this meant
that evangelicals were now indeed the 'mainstream' in American
religious life is both dependent upon one's own definitions and the
evidence which the future will produce.

To return to the beginning: revivals are uniquely American.
They come from deep, often inarticulate sources of emotion and conviction. They take different directions, assume different configura-
tions, reshuffle the table on which the players of religious faith
are placed.

The one we have looked at now in these pages is not yet
over. The academics are locked into permanent battle positions,
mediators shuffling back and forth, but with no signs of even an
armistice yet visible. The popular religion dimension continues, al-
beit with somewhat diminished appeal due to the oversell of some
of the slick promoters, the diminishing of stature of Bill Gothard
and Anita Bryant, and the growing evangelical acceptance of some
of the earlier, more bold expressions of born againism now accepted as normal, even a tad dull. And no one knows where the
political dimension of the 70's revival could lead. The power, the
technical proficiency, the convictions of the holders fast all suggest they are here for a long time and that politicians and religious leaders alike will have to accomodate themselves to the report cards and target lists of the times.

So, we return to where we began. The American revival is
a unique contribution to Protestant life and thought. It has maintained its vigor and power because its message met the felt needs
of so many Americans over its two and one half centuries of existence in this country. It has had to face the age-old problems of
holding on to its central core of affirmations about repentance,
conversion and the new life in the midst of enormous social, economic, and scientific change. Throughout all of the revivals, the
focus has remained on the harvest of souls through the born again
experience.

Yet, as I have argued in these pages, the revival of the late 70s has had to make many changes, adapt new techniques, find fresh means of appeal to stay afloat in a society (and world) which is increasingly indifferent to its otherworldly perspective. It may well be as Andrew Greeley and others have argued that ours is an age no less "religious" nor more "secular" than any other. This is a genuine chicken and egg dilemma. The revival of the 70s, however, to risk a prediction in these last paragraphs, is qualitatively different from its predecessors. For the first time three major changes from earlier revivals were made. First, the long standing battle between holders fast and pressers on broke out into full public debate. So serious has the battle become that it seems fair to conclude it cannot in the foreseeable future be resolved. We may thus see the end of the traditional scholarly leadership for revivals so much a part of their history.

Secondly, never before has the attractiveness of slick, success-oriented techniques of evangelism been so available and so widely adapted by those caught up in the revivalism of popular religion. We have no way of determining the numbers, but it seems reasonable to assert that a large number of seekers may well have rejected seeking the born again experience because of its razzmatazz, just as millions of others were drawn to it for that reason. Hence, there exists the very real possibility that the depth and profundity of a genuine conversion may well be submerged in electronic, celebrity-oriented outreach. We may never again see a revivalist like Jonathan Edwards, George Whitefield, Charles G. Finney or Dwight L. Mcody.

Thirdly, the instant success of the holders fast in the world of politics may well tend to bring on something of a major religious division within the populace. Talk of "christianizing America" may bring some to their feet with cheers, but others to their feet to resist. Politics as revival has been tried and until 1980 been resisted in America. One is apprehensive about what might happen if the battle persists.

And the more is the pity because neither the holders-pressers battle, nor the hoopala of electronic evangelism nor the political crusaders must necessarily destroy the best of revivalist appeal. The strength of that tradition's affirmations should be, but obviously has not yet become, its capacity to lead the searcher beyond separating the sacred from the secular towards recognizing the new life as one of indefinite growth. For all concerned: scholars, preachers, office seekers, laity, the power of the born again could be restored once the experience is defined as that of a pilgrimage. It is not an entrance into a safe harbor, but rather the beginnings of a voyage into the unknown.

It is at this point that healing for the immediate future of revivalism is the most in need. Travelling as a pilgrim, the seeker can move out of her or his labeled box of "evangelical" or "mainliner". The lures of the media, the antagonism over evangelism versus social outreach, the battles over hermeneutics, the contests between the sexes will continue to hold center stage. But if the evangelical voice is to speak again in the manner it once did, it will have to recover the sense of the continuing presence of God in our midst, in the midst of all searchers. That leaves those in their labeled boxes, and other outside critics, with the responsibility to accept the fact that it is their responsibility to revitalize their commitments. Without an infallible how-to-be-born-again manual as their guide, they can find again the renewing strength of recommitment and ways to share this with others. So long as the message is the good news of Immanuel, that God is with us, the future is open for healing and reunification.

APPENDIX I

THE CHICAGO DECLARATION
NOVEMBER, 1973

As evangelical Christians commited to the Lord Jesus Christ and the full authority of the Word of God, we affirm that God lays total claim upon the lives of his people. We cannot, therefore, separate our lives in Christ from the situation in which God has placed us in the United States and the world.

We confess that we have not acknowledged the complete claims of God on our lives.

We acknowledge that God requires love. But we have not demonstrated the love of God to those suffering social abuses.

We acknowledge that God requires justice. But we have not proclaimed or demonstrated his justice to an unjust American society. Although the Lord calls us to defend the social and economic rights of the poor and the oppressed, we have mostly remained silent. We deplore the historic involvement of the church in America with racism and the conspicuous responsibility of the evangelical community for perpetuating the personal attitudes and institutional structures that have divided the body of Christ along color lines. Further, we have failed to condemn the exploitation of racism at home and abroad by our economic system.

Reprinted from Ronald J. Sider, ed., The Chicago Declaration (Carol Stream, Creation House, 1974), cover page, pp. 1-3.

We affirm that God abounds in mercy and that he forgives all who repent and turn from their sins. So we call our fellow evangelical Christians to demonstrate repentence in a Christian discipleship that confronts the social and political injustice of our nation.

We must attack the materialism of our culture and the maldistribution of the nation's wealth and services. We recognize that as a nation we play a crucial role in the imbalance and injustice of international trade and development. Before God and a billion hungry neighbors, we must rethink our values regarding our present standard of living and promote more just acquisition and distribution of the world's resources.

We acknowledge our Christian responsibilities of citizenship. Therefore, we must challenge the misplaced trust of the nation in economic and military might -- a proud trust that promotes a national pathology of war and violence which victimizes our neighbors at home and abroad. We must resist the temptation to make the nation and its institutions objects of near-religious loyalty.

We acknowledge that we have encouraged men to prideful domination and women to irresponsible passivity. So we call both men and women to mutual submission and active discipleship.

We proclaim no new gospel, but the gospel of our Lord Jesus Christ, who, through the power of the Holy Spirit, frees people from sin so that they might praise God through works of righteousness.

By this declaration, we endorse no political ideology or party, but call our nation's leaders and people to that righteousness which exalts a nation.

We make this declaration in the biblical hope that Christ is coming to consummate the Kingdom and we accept his claim on our total discipleship till he comes.

NOTES

PART ONE -- CHAPTER I

1. William G. McLoughlin, Jr., Revivals, Awakenings, and Reform: An Essay on Religion and Social Change in America (Chicago: University of Chicago Press, 1978), p. xiii.

2. Ibid.

3. Richard Quebedeaux, The Worldly Evangelicals (New York: Harper and Row, 1978), is a typology survey; Robert K. Johnston, Evangelicals at an Impasse (Atlanta: John Knox Press, 1979), is a theological survey.

4. See Godfrey Hodgson, America in Our Time: From World War II to Nixon -- What Happened and Why (New York: Random, Vintage, 1978); William L. O'Neill, Coming Apart: An Informal History of America in the 1960s (New York: Times Books, Quadrangle, 1971); Lawrence S. Wittner, Cold War America: From Hiroshima to Watergate (New York: Praeger, 1974).

5. As claimed by its unofficial historian, Richard Quebedeaux, Worldly, p. xi.

6. Jeremy Rifkin and Ted Howard, The Changing Order: God in the Age of Scarcity (New York: G.P. Putnam's Sons, 1979) pp. 233-72.

7. John Dillenberger and Claude Welch, Protestant Christianity Interpreted Through Its Development (New York: Charles Scribner's Sons, 1954), p. 97. A lucid, contemporary definition is in Morris Inch, The Evangelical Imperative (Philadelphia: The Westminster Press, 1978).

8. For further discussion see the article on this by Donald W. Dayton in the Union Seminary Quarterly Review, Winter, 1977, pp. 73-4.

9. Johnston, Impasse, ch. 1; Inch, Evangelical Imperative, ch. 5.

10. See Richard Quebedeaux, I Found It: The Story of Bill Bright and the Campus Crusade (New York: Harper and Row, 1979), which has information on several of these groups.

11. In the American Historical Review, December, 1977, p. 1215, emphasis his.

CHAPTER II

1. Carl F.H. Henry, Remaking the Modern Mind (Grand Rapids: Eerdmans, 1946), pp. 146, 265-66, 300.

2. A sermon by Billy Graham, "We Need Revival, " in Graham, Revival in Our Time (Wheaton : Van Kampen Press, 1951), p. 75; Marshall Frady, Billy Graham: A Biography of American Righteousness (Boston: Little, Brown & Co., 1979), pp. 197-201.

3. Still the best study is Donald B. Meyer, The Positive Thinkers (Garden City: Doubleday, 1965; rev. ed., New York, Pantheon Books, 1980).

4. An editorial, Christianity Today, 15 October 1956, and more accessible in Frank E. Gaebelein, ed., A Christianity Today Reader (Westwood, NJ: Spire Books, 1968), pp. 13-6.

5. McLoughlin, Billy Graham (New York: The Ronald Co., 1960), pp. 148-51; John Pollock, Billy Graham: The Authorized Biography (Grand Rapids: Zondervan, 1966), pp. 61-8; New York Times, 17 December 1954, p. 3; United Evangelical Action, February, 1955, p. 13; Frady, Graham, pp. 297-305.

6. Christianity Today, 20 June 1960, pp. 788-89.

CHAPTER III

1. Sydney E. Ahlstrom, "The Moral and Theological Revolution of the 1960s and Its Implications for American History," in Herbert J. Bass, ed., The State of American History (New York: Time Books, Quadrangle, 1970), pp. 100, 101, 103; Ahlstrom, "The Radical Turn in Theology and Ethics: Why It Occurred in the 1960s," The Annals of the American Academy of Political and Social Science, January, 1970, p. 3; John Brooks, "A Clean Break With the Past," American Heritage, August, 1970 passim.

2. Hodgson, America, p. 306 and ch. 16; Morris Dickstein, Garden of Eden: American Culture in the Sixties (New York: Basic Books, 1977).

3. Hodgson, America, ch. 16; Theodore C. White, The Making of a President, 1968 (New York: Atheneum Books, 1969), the first chapters.

4. Well documented accounts are in Hodgson, America, ch. 19 and White, President, 1968.

5. See the editorials and articles in Christianity Today during these years; they are too numerous to cite here.

6. For instance, "The Communist Issue Today," Christianity Today, 22 May 1961, p. 23; L. Nelson Bell, "Christian Race Relation," ibid., 19 July 1963, p. 1027; "Racial Integration" in Robert Campbell, ed., Spectrum of Protestant Beliefs (Milwaukee: The Bruce Publishing Co., 1968), p. 69; "What of Racial Intermarriage?" Christianity Today, 11 October 1963, pp. 26-8; Ilion T. Jones, "Enforced Christianity?" ibid., 10 April 1964, pp. 429-32.

7. Ibid., 12 February 1965, p. 511; 21 May 1965, p. 894; 19 July 1965, p. 1141.

8. Ibid., 7 January 1966, pp. 353-54.

9. See the editorials in Christianity Today, Eternity, Decision, and Moody Monthly on these topics, and especially Harold Berry, "The Quest for Peace," Moody Monthly, December, 1969, p. 34.

10. Printed sermon, "When Silence is Yellow," (Minneapolis: Billy Graham Evangelistic Association) Summer, no. 156, pp. 1-8.

11. Alan Levy, God Bless You Real, Good: My Crusades with Billy Graham (New York: Simon and Schuster, 1969), pp. 76-8; John Pollock, Crusades: Twenty Years with Billy Graham (Minneapolis: World Wide Pubs., 1969), pp. 277-78; Decision, March, 1969, pp. 8-9; Frady, Graham, pp. 421-33.

12. Levy, God Bless You, p. 82; Edward B. Fiske, "The Closest Thing to a White House Chaplain," New York Magazine, 8 June 1969, p. 111; Pollock, Crusades, p. 278; Frady, Graham, pp. 421-33.

13. See "Graham Denounces Dissenters," Christian Century, 17 May 1967, p. 645; Newsweek, 10 June 1969, p. 63; New York Times, 24 June 1979, p. 37.

14. Henry, "Demythologizing the Evangelicals," Christianity Today, 13 September 1968, p. 1182; "Plight of the Evangelicals," ibid., 5 July 1968, p. 985.

15. Henry, Faith at the Frontiers (Chicago: Moody Press, 1969), p. 157, ch. 11, 13; Mark Hatfield, Not Quite So Simple (New York: Harper and Row, 1968) and Conflict and Conscience (Waco: Word Books, 1971); John B. Anderson, Between Two Worlds (Grand Rapids: Zondervan, 1970); Robert G. Clouse, et al, eds., Protest and Politics: Christianity and Contemporary Affairs (Greenwood, SC: The Attic Press, 1968); Will D. Campbell and James Y. Holloway, eds., Up to Our Steeples in Politics (New York: Paulist Press, 1970).

CHAPTER IV

1. As quoted by Robert Fitch in Christian Century, 1 February 1967, p. 139.

2. Reprinted in Armin Rappaport and Richard Traina, eds., Present in the Past (New York: Macmillan, 1972), pp. 493–96.

3. Minneapolis Star, 12 December 1971, p. 148.

4. Graham, "Three American Illusions," Christianity Today, 19 December 1969, pp. 260–62; see the Billy Graham Evangelistic Association sermons by Graham and other team members, no. 183, 184, 187, 188, 190, 191, 192, 193; Decision, March, 1968, p. 2   and July, 1971; Time, 4 January 1971, p. 3.

5. The speech is reprinted in Christianity Today, 31 July 1970, pp. 988–89.   See also Lowell D. Streiker and Gerald S. Strober, Religion and the New Majority (New York: Association Press, 1972), pp. 70–7.

6. Quebedeaux, The Young Evangelicals (New York, Harper and Row, 1974), pp. 120.   See this source for a full statement of purpose.

7. The Post American, Spring, 1972, pp. 9–10.

8. Ibid., p. 10; Quebedeaux, Young, pp. 84–5.   A different view is in Strieker and Strober, Religion, pp. 70–7.   See also Jim Wallis, Agenda for Biblical People (New York: Harper and Row, 1976).

9. Quebedeaux, Young, pp. 69–72; Quebedeaux, Worldly, pp. 85–90.

10. See the flyers signed by Howard and others, "Evangelicals for McGovern," printed at 2026 N. Broad St., Philadelphia, PA.   See also editorial in The Reformed Journal, November, 1972; James Armstrong, "The Case for McGovern," Christian Century, 1 November 1972, pp. 1096–098.

11. See their analysis in Commentary, January, 1973, pp. 43–50.

12. Quebedeaux, I Found It! See also Robert S. Ellwood, Jr., One Way: The Jesus Movement and Its Meaning (Englewood Cliffs: Prentice-Hall, 1973).

13. See the many articles and analyses throughout the year in Christianity Today, especially 19 January and 28 September 1973.

14. Ibid., 28 September 1973, p. 1314; Ron Sider, ed., The Chicago Declaration (Carol Stream: Creation House, 1974), p. 15.

15. Quebedeaux, Worldly, pp. 59-61 and the many stories in the 1974 issues of Christianity Today.

16. Ibid., 21 December 1973, p. 370; Sider, ed., Chicago passim.

17. See Appendix I and a very complete account by many of the participants in Sider, Chicago.

18. Quebedeaux, Worldly, p. 146.

19. See the critiques by Kurt Back, Beyond Words (Baltimore: Penquin Books, 1973); Edwin Schur, The Awareness Trap (New York : Times Books, Quadrangle, 1976); Christopher Lasch, The Culture of Narcissism: American Life in an Age of Diminishing Expectations (New York: W.W. Norton, 1978).

PART TWO -- CHAPTER V

1. Ahlstrom, "The Traumatic Years: American Religion and Culture in the 60s and 70s," Theology Today, January, 1980, pp. 505-22.

2. McLoughlin, Revivals, p. xiii.

3. Donald Tinder, "Why the Evangelical Uprising?" Christianity Today, 21 October 1977, pp. 76-8.

4. E.J. Carnell, The Case for Orthodox Theology (Philadelphia: Westminster Press, 1959); Donald G. Bloesch, The Evangelical Renaissance (Grand Rapids: Eerdmans, 1973); Millard Erickson, The New Evangelical Theology (Old Tappen, NJ: Fleming H. Revell Co., 1968); Ronald Nash, The New Evangelicalism (Grand Rapids: Zondervan, 1963); David F. Wells and John D. Woodbridge, eds., The Evangelicals: What They Believe, Who They Are, Where They Are Changing (Nashville: Abingdon, 1975).

5. Johnston, Impasse, p. 2; Clark Pinnock, "Three Views of the Bible in Contemporary Theology," Jack Rogers, ed., Biblical Authority (Waco: Word Books, 1977), pp. 47-73; Robert Webber, Common Roots (Grand Rapids: Zondervan, 1978).

6. Frank E. Gaebelein, ed., Christianity Today (Old Tappan, NJ: Fleming H. Revell Co., 1968), pp. 13-6; Quebedeaux, Worldly, p. 33.

7. Inch, Evangelical Imperative, ch. 5; on errors; see Johnston, Impasse, pp. 19-22, 36-7; James C. Vanderkam, "Inerrancy, Princeton, and Orthodoxy," The Reformed Journal, April, 1980, p. 18.

8. Henry, "The God of the Bible versus Naturalism," Edwin H. Rian, ed., Christianity and World Revolution (New York, Harper and Row, 1963), p. 234; Johnston, Impasse, ch. 2; Pinnock, "Three Views," pp. 47-73.

9. Jack Rogers and Donald McKim, The Authority and Interpretation of the Bible: An Historical Approach (New York: Harper and Row, 1979).

10. Edwin Young, Thy Word is Truth (Grand Rapids: Eerdmans, 1957), p. 71; Gordon Clark, "How May I Know the Bible is Inspired?" Howard V. Vos, ed., Can I Trust the Bible? (Chicago: Moody Press, 1963), pp. 9-31, especially p. 27.

11. See the documentation in Ina J. Kau, "Feminists in the American Evangelical Movement" (M.A. thesis, Pacific School of Religion, Berkeley, CA, 1977).

12. Quebedeaux, Worldly, p. 88; Paul Jewett, Man as Male and Female (Grand Rapids: Eerdmans, 1975), pp. 137-41 passim; Letha Scanzoni and Nancy Hardesty, All We're Meant To Be (Waco: Word Books, 1974).

13. Harold Lindsell, The Battle for the Bible (Grand Rapids: Zondervan, 1976), pp. 34-5, 40-71, 162, 182.

14. Johnston, Impasse, p. 21.

15. Lindsell, Battle, p. 20.

16. Johnston, Impasse, pp. 18-47.

17. Francis Schaffer's magnus opus is How Should We Then Live? (Old Tappen, NJ: Fleming H. Revell Co., 1977); see a critique in Thomas V. Morris, Francis Schaeffer's Apologetics: A Critique (Chicago: Moody Press, 1976). Among his most responsible critics are Jack Rogers, Reformed Journal, May, 1977, pp. 12-5, and June, 1977, pp. 15-9; and Clark Pinnock, "Schaefferism as a World View," Sojourners, July, 1977, pp. 32-5.

18. Dayton, "The Battle over the Bible: Renewing the Inerrancy Debate," Christian Century, 10 November 1976, pp. 976–80;
see the critics of Dayton in ibid., 2 March 1977, pp. 198–99;
Johnston, Impasse, p. 161.

19. Henry, "The War of the Word," The New Review of Books
and Religion, September, 1976, p. 7; Henry, Evangelicals in Search
of an Identity (Waco: Word Books, 1977), p. 5; Johnston, Impasse,
pp. 161–63.

20. Christianity Today, 4 November 1977, pp. 249–50. A small
but influential group of irenically-minded evangelical scholars met
in May, 1977 in Chicago, issuing a call for evangelicalism to return to its roots in historic Christianity. See Robert Webber and
Donald Bloesch, eds., The Orthodox Evangelicals (Nashville: Thomas
Nelson, 1978).

21. Lindsell, The Bible in the Balance (Grand Rapids:
Zondervan, 1979); Dayton, "The 'Battle for the Bible' Rages On,"
Theology Today, April, 1980, pp. 79–84.

22. Kenneth Kantzer, "Evangelicals and the Inerrancy Question," Christianity Today, 18 April 1979, pp. 900–05; also Stephen
T. Davis, The Debate About the Bible: Inerrancy versus Infallibility (Philadelphia: Westminster Press, 1977).

23. See news items in Christianity Today, 20 July 1979,
p. 1058–060 and 1692–693.

24. Henry, "Evangelicals: Out of the Closet but Going Nowhere?" Christianity Today, 4 January 1980, p. 17; see also "On
Inerrancy, Princeton, and Orthodoxy," Reformed Journal, April,
1980, pp. 18–30.

CHAPTER VI

1. Dayton, Discovering an Evangelical Heritage (New York:
Harper and Row, 1976), ch. 8.

2. Marty, Context, 15 July 1977, pp. 4–5; Johnston, Impasse,
ch. 3 contains exhaustive documentation.

3. Johnston, Impasse, p. 49 and ch. 3.

4. As compiled by Letha Scanzoni, "The Early Feminists and
the Bible," Christianity Today, 2 February 1973, pp. 10–5; and
Miriam G. Moran, ed., What You Should Know About Women's Lib
(New Canaan, CT: Keats, 1974), pp. 8–17.

5. In the Post-American, May, 1975, p. 12; Elisabeth Elliot, Let Me Be a Woman (Wheaton: Tyndale House, 1976), pp. 17, 20, 22, and ch. 7; Pat Brooks, Daughter of the King (Carol Stream: Creation House, 1975), pp. 35-6; Johnston, Impasse, pp. 53-5.

6. Hardesty and Scanzoni, All, pp. 17-22.

7. Jewett, Man as Male and Female, Part III; Scanzoni, "The Great Chain of Being and the Chain of Command," The Reformed Journal, October, 1976, pp. 14-8; Hardesty and Scanzoni, All, pp. 23-4; Virginia Ramey Mollenkott, Men, Women and the Bible (Nashville: Abingdon, 1977), ch. 6; Johnston, Impasse, p. 51.

8. Elliot, Let, pp. 115-16, 126-27, 128-29, 139-40.

9. Brooks, Daughters, ch. 4-5.

10. Hardesty and Scanzoni, All, ch. 5.

11. Mollenkott, Men, Women, pp. 12-21; Mollenkott, "Women and the Bible," The Reformed Journal, February, 1976, p. 25; see also Rachel C. Wahlberg, Jesus According to a Woman (New York: Paulist Press, 1975).

12. Elliot, Let, p. 163.

13. Hardesty and Scanzoni, All, ch. 6; Richard and Joyce Boldrey, Chauvinist or Feminist? Paul's View of Women (Grand Rapids: Baker Book House, 1976).

14. Johnston, Impasse, p. 52.

15. Ibid., p. 54.

16. Ibid., pp. 69-75.

CHAPTER VII

1. Johnston, Impasse, p. 95.

2. Ibid., p. 96; see his documentation.

3. See a profile by Carol Greenberg Felsenthal, "Phyllis Schlafly is One Tough Mother," Chicago, June, 1978, pp. 128-34.

4. Phyllis Schlafly, The Power of the Positive Woman (New York: Harcourt, Brace, Jovanovich, 1977), see especially pp. 60-1, 213.

5. Specific arguments of hers are in "The Phyllis Schlafly Report," June, 1974; September, 1974; November, 1974; December, 1974; National Courier, 7 October 1975, p. 28; Newsweek, 7 November 1977, p. 41. See also the debate on ERA in America, 17 May 1975, pp. 374-81.

6. Some readers may wonder why Lutherans were chosen as spokespersons. I found their article was among the most responsible cases available at the time of the debate addressing itself specifically to evangelicals' questions.

7. Lutheran Women, November, 1975, p. 18; Robert M. Williams, "Woman Against Women," Saturday Review, 7 June 1977, pp. 7-13ff; see also the articles on ERA in The Daughters of Sarah.

8. See the statistics in Johnston, Impasse, p. 115; Quebedeaux, Worldly, pp. 128-31.

9. Johnston, Impasse, p. 121.

10. Time, 26 December 1977, p. 54; Anita Bryant, The Anita Bryant Story (Old Tappan, NJ: Fleming H. Revell Co., 1977), pp. 42, 53-5; Johnston, Impasse, p. 121.

11. Lewis Smedes, Sex for Christians (Grand Rapids: Eerdmans, 1976), pp. 73-6.

12. Mollenkott and Scanzoni, Is the Homosexual My Neighbor: Another Christian View (New York: Harper and Row, 1978); see Johnston's critique in Impasse, pp. 129-44.

13. Mollenkott and Scanzoni, Is, p. 71.

14. Quebedeaux, Worldly, pp. 128-31.

15. Johnston, Impasse, p. 143.

16. Marty, Context, p. 2; Hatfield, "Abortion: A Legislator Speaks, Reformed Journal, September, 1973, pp. 11-4.

17. An interview in the Minneapolis Tribune, 26 March 1978, p. 9A. The most extensive anti-abortion discussion by an evangelical is H.O.J. Brown, Death Before Life (Nashville: Thomas Nelson, 1978). See also the extended theological discussion in Dialog, Spring, 1978.

18. Tim and Beverly La Haye, The Act of Marriage (Grand Rapids: Zondervan, 1976), pp. 235-27.

19. Salter O. Spitzer and Carlyle L. Saylor, eds., Birth Control and the Christian (Wheaton: Tyndale House, 1969).

PART THREE -- CHAPTER VIII

1. Peter W. Williams, Popular Religion in America: Symbolic Change and the Modernization Process in Historical Perspective, (Englewood Cliffs, NJ: Prentice-Hall, 1980), pp. 17-8.

2. Albert J. Menendez, Religion at the Polls (Philadelphia: The Westminster Press, 1977), p. 189; Donald Meyer, The Positive Thinkers: Religion as Pop Psychology from Mary Baker Eddy to Oral Roberts (New York: Pantheon Books, 1980), pp. 336-47.

3. The Minneapolis Tribune, 5 March 1970, p. 5.

4. Robert Tapp, "On the Rise of Demoltheology," Christian Century, 3 February 1971, pp. 153-56.

5. Dean Kelley, Why Conservative Churches are Growing (New York: Harper and Row, 1972). Marty quipped that it could just as well have been titled "Why Mainline Churches are Declining" since the material helped explain that too.

6. Marty, Context, 15 November 1977, based on a seven year study.

7. Quebedeaux, Young, pp. 102-09; Bruce Larson, Ask Me to Dance (Waco: Word Books, 1972); Bruce Larson and Keith Miller, Living the Adventure (Waco: Word Books, 1975).

CHAPTER IX

1. Minneapolis Tribune, 6 May 1977, p. 4B. One of the best recent bibliographies by a responsible, secular scholar on the sexual revolution is James Leslie McCarry, Human Sexuality (New York: Van Nostrand Reinhold, 1978, 3rd ed.), pp. 437-67. See also Christianity Today, 5 May 1978, p. 997; Minneapolis Tribune, 4 May 1978, p. 3A; Newsweek, 1 August 1977, pp. 46-7. An extended discussion is in Roger W. Libby and Robert Whitefield, eds., Marriage and Alternatives: Exploring Intimate Relationships (Glenview, IL: Scott, Foresman, 1977, 2nd ed.).

2. The most complete analysis is Wilfred Bockelman, Gothard: The Man and his Ministry: An Evaluation (Milford, MI: Mott Media, 1976).

3. Wesley Norton, Captivated by Christ (Christian Literature Crusade: Fort Washington, PA: 1956).

4. Bockelman, Gothard, p. 149. See the story on Gothard by Willard Thorkelson in the National Courier, 10 December 1976, p. 9A and another story by Thorkelson in the Minneapolis Star, 6 November 1976, p. 5A.

5. Bockelman, Gothard, ch. 12.

6. Marty, Context, 15 August 1974 passim; ibid., 1 November 1974, pp. 4-5.

7. Stephen E. Smallman reviewing Bockelman in Christianity Today, 3 June 1977, p. 996.

8. J. Elmo Agrimson in Lutheran Standard, 1 October 1974, p. 20C. See also the story by Edward E. Plowman in Christianity Today, 25 May 1973, pp. 44-5.

9. Quebedeaux, Worldly, pp. 74-6.

10. Christianity Today, 8 August 1980, pp. 916-17.

CHAPTER X

1. "How 60,000 Women Feel About Religion and Morality," McCalls, May, 1978, pp. 12ff. The article includes statistics on "evangelicals' attitudes."

2. Mary Ryan, "American Women in the 1970s," reprinted in Thomas R. Frazier, ed., The Underside of American History (New York: Harcourt, Brace, Jovanovich, 1974) Vol. II, pp. 332-45; Marty, Context, 1 December 1976, p. 4.

3. Time, 14 March 1977, pp. 64, 67.

4. Ibid., p. 64.

5. Proverbs 5:19 and I Corinthians 7:4-5 (RSV).

6. Marabelle Morgan, Total Woman (New York: Pocket Books, 1975), pp. 132-33, 141.

7. Morgan, Woman, ch. 13 and Total Joy (Old Tappen, NJ: Fleming H. Revell Co., 1976), p. 204.

8. Joyce Maynard, "The Liberation of Total Woman," New York Times Magazine, 29 September 1975, pp. 54, 55; David Kucharsky, The Man From Plains: The Mind and Spirit of Jimmy Carter (New York: Harper and Row, Perennial Library, 1976), p. 78.

9. Jim Wallis, "Conversion," Sojourners, May, 1978, p. 12.

10. Patricia Gundry, Woman Be Free (Grand Rapids: Zondervan, 1978 passim.

11. Peggy Noll, book review of Morgan in National Courier, 20 February 1976, p. 19.

12. Joyce Maynard, "Liberation," United Methodist Response, December, 1976, p. 66.

13. "The Totalled Woman," The Wittenburg Door, August–September, 1975; John Scanzoni, "Authority in Christian Marriage," Reformed Journal, November, 1974, p. 34; Scanzoni, "Assertiveness for Christian Women," Christianity Today, 4 June 1976, p. 929.

14. See also Larry and Nordis Christenson, The Christian Couple (Minneapolis: Bethany Fellowship, 1978); Herbert J. and Fern Harrington Miles, Husband–Wife Equality (Old Tappan, NJ: Fleming H. Revell Co., 1978).

CHAPTER XI

1. Minneapolis Tribune, 20 April 1978, p. 88. Also a letter to me from Dr. Arno Q. Weniger, Jr., Executive Vice–President, American Association of Christian Schools, 8 June 1978. A more specific indictment of public schools is Elmer Towns, Have the Public Schools Had It? (Nashville: Thomas Nelson, 1974). He blames bungling bureaucracy, teachers' unions, undisciplined student behavior and free reign of drugs and physical violence.

2. Letter to me from Herman Van Schuyver, Director, National Association of Christian Schools, 23 May 1978.

3. Nicholas Wolterstorff, "Can Non–Public Christian Schools Be Justified?" Reformed Journal, April, 1978, pp. 13–7. Among Gaebelein's many books, see especially The Pattern of God's Truth (Chicago: Moody Press, 1968).

4. Wolterstorff, "Christian Schools," p. 14.

5. Ibid., p. 15.

6. Ibid., p. 16.

7. Ibid.

8. Ibid., p. 17. See also a pamphlet with extensive scriptural proof text support by Dr. Paul Carter, "A Christian Philosophy of

Education," (Hialiah, FL: American Association of Christian Schools, 1975).

9. "Boom in Protestant Schools," U.S. News and World Report, 8 October 1978, pp. 44-6.

10. "The Phyllis Schlafly Report," November, 1976 and December, 1976. Wolterstorff, "Christian Schools," p. 14 is less pessimistic about this.   See also the news story on Christian schools in Christianity Today, 20 December 1977 and "The Religion of Humanism in Public Schools," in The Barbara M. Morris Report (Ellicott City, MD., 1976) and a pamphlet by Morris, "Why Are You Losing Your Children?" (Ellicott City, MD., received by me in 1978).

11. "Family Renewal," a newpaper of Christian Family Renewal, Clovis, CA., n.d., vol. I, no. 1; Current, 19 April 1978, pp. 7, 11.

12. Current, 3 May 1978, p. 5.

CHAPTER XII

1. Quebedeaux, Worldly, p. 132.

2. Minneapolis Star, 17 February 1978, p. 14B.   The New York Times picked up the trend as early as 9 March 1975, pp. 1, 33; Kucharsky, "The Year of the Evangelical, 1976," Christianity Today, 22 October 1976, pp. 80-1; Minneapolis Star, 30 October 1976, p. 4A on Novak; C. Peter Wegner, "How Christian Is America?" Christianity Today, 3 December 1976, pp. 276-80; "A Time for Renewal in U.S. Churches," U.S. News and World Report, 11 April 1977, pp. 54-69; the NAE story in the Minneapolis Tribune, 14 March 1978 and 23 February 1978, pp. 1B, 4B.

3. See McLoughlin, "Revivalism," in Edwin Scott Gaustad, ed., The Rise of Adventism (New York: Harper and Row, 1974), pp. 125ff.

4. U.S. News and World Report, 11 April 1977, p. 61.   See also ibid., pp. 56-60, this estimate seems somewhat high in my judgment.

5. Marty's review of Quebedeaux's Worldly Evangelicals in Christian Century, 4 October 1978, p. 926. A similar critique is Virginia Stem Owens, The Total Image: Or Selling Jesus in the Modern Age (Grand Rapids: Eerdmans, 1980), p. 37.

6. U.S. News and World Report, 11 April 1977, p. 61 also pp. 56-60; Kucharsky, The Man from Plains, p. 81.

7. "Bringing the Word," New York Times Book Review, 3 March 1978, pp. 51ff; Publisher's Weekly, 14 March 1977, pp. 82-3; Christian Century, 18 May 1977, pp. 469-70; Marty, Context, 1 June 1966, p. 5.

8. Quebedeaux, Worldly, pp. 69-70; Douglas Mack, "Popular Religious Books for Public Libraries," Library Journal, 1 June 1977, pp. 1243-250; Christianity Today, 21 April 1978, p. 936.

9. John Garvey, "Religious Publishing in America," Commonweal, 28 April 1978, p. 282; Christian Century, 17 May 1978, p. 523.

10. Garvey, "Publishing," p. 283.

11. Dwayne Wells, "The Jesus Mania," Saturday Review, 17 September 1977, p. 17; see also the "Twin Cities Christian Business Directory, 1977," p. 3.

12. Marty, Context, 1 December 1977, p. 3. The National Council of Churches, a one page flyer, "A Call to Action by the NCC on the Christian Yellow Pages," 1977. Further discussion is also in The Humanist, January-February, 1978, p. 54.

13. Wells, "The Jesus Mania," p. 17; Marty, Context, 1 October 1977, p. 4; Christian Century, 12 April 1978, pp. 382-83; "Old Time Religion Reaches the Masses," Christian Life, January, 1977, p. 17ff.

14. Quebedeaux, Worldly, pp. 106, 149-52; Johnston, Impasse, pp.. 91-4, 115. See also the most complete compendium of evangelical popular religion in William Proctor, The Born-Again Christian Catalog: A Complete Sourcebook for Evangelicals (New York: M. Evans and Company, 1979), pp. 239-41.

15. Owens, Total Image, pp. 19-20, 23.

16. Ibid., p. 27.

17. Scott Hessek, "Christianity and the Supermedia," Christian Life, January, 1977, p. 75.

18. Move That Mountain (Plainfield, NJ: Logos International, 1976), p. 106 and ch. 4-15. Both CBN (Christian Broadcast Network) and PTL (Praise the Lord) publish paperback books of inspiration and instruction.

19. Flyer from PTL, n.d., received by me in 1979.

20. Wall Street Journal, 19 May 1978, pp. 1, 15; New York Times, 10 February 1980, p. 10E; Owens, Total Image, pp. 33-4.

21. Proctor, Catalog, pp. 242-49.

22. New York Times, 10 1980, p. 10E.

23. Marty, "The Electronic Church," in ELIM: Missouri in Perspective, 27 March 1978, p. 5; Marty, Context, 1 February 1978, p. 1; Thorkelson, Minneapolis Star, 30 June 1978, p. 28.

24. Henry, "Moving on the Media Frontier," Christianity Today, 10 September 1976, pp. 244-45; Edward Berknow, "The Old Time Gospel Hour and the Fundamentalist Paradox," Christian Century, 29 March 1978, p. 337; James A. Taylor, "Progeny of Programmers: Evangelical Religion and the Television Age," ibid., 20 April 1977, pp. 379-82 and the letters critical of this article in ibid., 14 September 1977, pp. 788-90.

25. Owens, Total Image, pp. 81-2.

26. Emma R. Talen, "Hustling Religion," The Reformed Journal, May, 1978, pp. 5-6; Steven Hortega, "H-E-R-E-'S Christian Show Biz!" Eternity, May, 1978, pp. 31-6.

27. Henry, Identity, p. 78. See also the book on the celebrities published by Creation House.

PART FOUR -- CHAPTER XIII

1. For an excellent discussion, see the essay by William Lee Miller, "American Religion and American Political Attitudes," in James Ward Smith and A. Leland Jamison, eds., Religious Perspectives in American Culture (Princeton: Princeton University Press, 1961), pp. 81-118. On Goldwater see Jorstad, The Politics of Doomsday (Nashville, Abingdon Press, 1970), pp. 98-103.

2. So went the general public attitude of that year, well exemplified by Kenneth A. Briggs, Religion Editor, New York Times, in an article in Christian Century, 12 May 1976, pp. 452-54; James Wooton, Dasher: The Roots and Rising of Jimmy Carter (New York: Warner Books, 1978), p. 33.

3. Printed in the article by Norman Mailer, "The Search for Carter," New York Times Magazine, 26 September 1976, p. 20. See also James M. Wall, "Words of Faith from Jimmy Carter," Christian Century, 17 January 1979, pp. 38-9; Wayne Boulton, "The Riddle of Romans 13," Christian Century, 15 September 1976, pp. 758-61.

4. Carter, Why Not the Best? (New York: Bantam Books, 1976), pp. 3, 167.

5. In the Christian Century, 1-8 August 1979, pp. 747-48.

6. Richard G. Hutcheson, Jr., "Jimmy Carter's Moral Presidency," Christian Century, 21 November 1979, pp. 1155–164. For evangelical criticism see John Anderson, "Faith, Virtue and Honor are not Enough," Christianity Today, 3 November 1978, pp. 150–56; Henry, "Evangelical Profits and Losses," Christian Century, 25 January 1978, pp. 69–70. Excellent political evaluation is in "The Presidential Watch" an ongoing series by John Osborn in The New Republic.

CHAPTER XIV

1. W.J. Bennett and Terry Eastland, "The 'New Right' Christians," Wall Street Journal, 17 September 1980, p. 1; Newsweek, 15 September 1980, p. 31.

2. Stan Hastey and Warner Ragsdale, "Right Religion: Right Politics," Home Missions, September/October, 1980, pp. 68–9; American Jewish Committee, "The New Right," (1980), pp. 1–5.

3. Ibid. See also Jorstad, The Politics of Moralism: The New Christian Right in American Life (Minneapolis: Augsburg Publishing House, 1981), ch. 9.

4. Newsweek, 15 September 1980, p. 29; Minneapolis Star, 25 August 1980, p. 4A and 1 November 1980, p. 1C; Hastey and Ragsdale, "Right Religion," p. 69.

5. American Jewish Committee, "The New Right," passim. This is an outstanding, brief, objective summary of the movement.

6. Robert Zwier and Richard Smith, "Christian Politics and the 'New Right'," Christian Century, 8 October 1980 passim; interview by Bill Moyers of Vigurie on Bill Moyers' Journal, 28 September 1980; Newsweek, 15 September 1980, pp. 27–31.

7. As claimed by Quebedeaux, Worldly, p. xi–xii. For a good sampling of church leaders' opinions see issues of Marty, Context.

CHAPTER XV

1. As told to talk show emcee, George Otis and reprinted in Christianity Today, 2 July 1976, p. 1047.

2. Ibid. See also Helene Von Damm, ed., Sincerely, Ronald Reagan (New York: Berkley Books, 1976), pp. 88–98.

3. Alan Crawford, Thunder on the Right: The New Right and the Politics of Resentment (New York: Pantheon Books, 1980); James Q. Wilson, "Reagan and the Republican Revival," Commentary, October, 1980, pp. 25-32.

4. Jorstad, The Politics of Moralism, ch. 11; Marty, Context, 15 July 1980, pp. 1-5.

5. Newsweek, 15 September 1980, pp. 31-2; Minneapolis Star, 25 August 1980, pp. 8A, 12A.

6. See the issues of 1979 and 1980 of Billing's monthly newsletter, Alert.

7. Minneapolis Star, 7 November 1980, p. 6A; Minneapolis Tribune, 11 November 1980, p. 7B and 18 November 1980, p. 8A; New York Times, 10 November 1980, p. 12.

8. Christianity Today, 19 September 1980, p. 1071; Christian Century, 24 September 1980, p. 872; see Robison's monthly newsletter, Life's Answers, October, 1980, pp. 7-8.

9. Human Events, 11 October 1980, p. 12.

10. As heard on Bill Moyer's Journal, 28 September 1980 and reprinted in Newsweek, 10 November 1980, p. 76.

11. New York Times, 4 October 1980, p. 9 and 10 October 1980, p. 14D; Tom F. Driver, "Hating Jews for Jesus' Sake," Christianity and Crisis, 24 November 1980, pp. 325ff.

12. New York Times, 11 October 1980, p. 8.

13. New York Times, 10 October 1980, p. 14D.

14. Newsweek, 10 November 1976, p. 76.

15. Minneapolis Star, 6 November 1980, p. 23A; New York Times, 5 November 1980, p. 19A and 6 November 1980, p. 29A.